Blueprint of a GOD Man

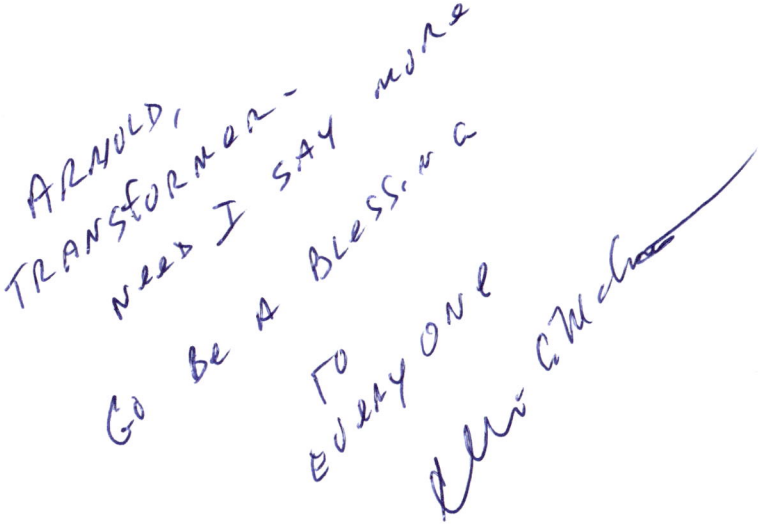

ARNOLD,
TRANSFORMER-
NEED I SAY MORE
GO BE A BLESSING
TO
EVERYONE
Ellis C McCarthy

Ellis C. McCarthy

Unless otherwise indicated, all scripture quotations, references and definitions are from the Authorized King James Version © 1987; The New King James Version © 1982 by Thomas Nelson, Inc.; The New International Version 1973, 1978, 1984 by International Bible Society by the Zondervan Corporation; The Amplified Bible Old Testament © 1962, 1964, 1965, 1987 by the Zondervan Corporation; The Amplified New Testament © 1954, 1958, 1987 by the Lockman Foundation; The Message. Copyright © 1993, 1994, 1995, 1996, 2000, 2001, 2002. Used by permission of NavPress Publishing Group. All rights reserved; M.G. Easton M.A., D.D., Illustrated Bible Dictionary, Third Edition, published by Thomas Nelson, 1897; The Name Book © 1982, 1997 by Dorothy Astoria.

Blueprint OF A GOD Man

Ellis C. McCarthy Ministries
430 East 162nd Street #451
South Holland, Illinois 60473
ellismccarthy.org I blueprintofagodman.com

Copyright © 2015 Ellis C. McCarthy
ISBN # 978-1-943343-34-8

PublishAffordably.com
www.PublishAffordably.com I 773-783-2981

PASTOR JERRY MCQUAY

"We no longer live in the kind of world where the Apostle Paul said, "when I became a man, I put away childish things." (1 Corinthians 13:11, NKJV) How many guys even know the difference between men and boys? How can today's men understand the process of achieving real manhood?

There is no question that today men in America are often confused about their identity, uncertain as to what real manhood looks like, and worse yet, have no clue as to how to get there. My friend, Ellis McCarthy, has a heart to change that, and he writes from his own experience in helping other men to become the kind of man that God designed them to be. I hope you will not only read this book, but that you will find wisdom and help for your own life and for those that you influence, no matter what season you are in."

Jerry McQuay, Senior Pastor
Christian Life Center
Tinley Park, Illinois

Blueprint of a God Man

A Message From My Wife

For years I have seen the unique gift of Ellis ministering life into the wilted places of a man's heart. The beauty of it all is that it is befitting for all ages both young and old.

He has spoken over our children, but even more important, our children's children in the next generation—an inheritance that will never be forgotten.

I have seen Ellis on his face standing in the gap for men, not withholding crying out to the God he knows all so well. And yet I have seen him speaking on platforms with the same humble spirit.

Ellis has been chosen to "Prepare the Way" for men with and without fathers, to shift them into their destiny—to teach them Ecclesiastes 3 illuminating the essence of the times and seasons of their life.

"Blueprint of a God Man" is more than a book. It is a roadmap to your destiny.

Without a doubt heaven is rejoicing as Ellis embarks on

another milestone in his life, and I couldn't be more honored to be his help meet along the way.

~ All My Love,
Donna Y. McCarthy

DEDICATION

To my wife Donna, thank you for the inspiration you gave me to do what God had predestined. You not only encouraged me but continued to keep me focused on the purpose that was set. The words were in my mind but they were not translated on the paper. Just as water has to be primed in a well to start the water flow, you have been the primer for my heart.

When Adam woke up and God presented Eve to him, he felt something was missing he also knew that Eve was the missing thing to complete him. When God brought you to me, I knew, you were my completion. You are my help meet who God blessed me with and I am forever grateful.

To the men who have created the legacy which I live, and to the men that create new legacies of my bloodline every day.

The late Seth McCarty, Great Grandfather, known as a Minister of the Evening Light Saints

The late Roosevelt McCarthy, Grandfather, a Pastor

who worked alongside the founding fathers of the Churches of God in Christ

The late Bishop Dr. Samuel S. McCarthy, My father, an outstanding Church of God in Christ Bishop

Carlton McCarthy, Son, Church Financial Director

Spencer McCarthy, Grandson, future church leader

Samuel Lagunas, Grandson, future church leader

Kevin Hylton, and Enrique Lagunas, Son in-laws.

To my daughters, Taquia Hylton, Erika Lagunas, daughter in-law, Katija McCarthy, and granddaughter, Kennedy Hylton. You are the reason authentic manhood is so important to me. You deserve the best. If you don't know the best, you'll settle for less. So I have to set the standard which I expect you to have and demand. Never settle for less than the example I've tried to show you; even when I was learning on the job. I love you.

To my mother, Omega McCarthy, the greatest intercessor and prayer warrior I know. Thank you for teaching me to live by these scriptures: Jhn 3:16, Eph 4:32, Pro 3:5-6, and Ecc 12:13-14.

TABLE OF CONTENTS

Blueprint of a God Man

FOREWORD
APOSTLE DARYL O'NEIL

In every generation there are voices needed, seasoned with wisdom and experience to help men on their journey in this life. Ellis McCarthy is just such a voice and man for this and future generations.

In Blueprint of a God Man: Navigating the Seasons of Life, Ellis offers a unique look at the stages men journey through, often without help. He offers to us wisdom for progressing, growing and maturing according to God's plan for our lives.

I pray you will be inspired and transformed as you "Navigate" this resource.

Daryl O'Neil, Apostle
Ruach Covenant Church International
Chicago, Illinois

Blueprint of a GOD Man
INTRODUCTION

From very early in ministry, I had a real passion for seeing men developed to the point of fulfilling their God-given purpose. As I began to work with men, I recognized how far away from it they actually were. I even begin to evaluate myself and realized, "I am so far from where I want to be." I was even further away from where God wanted me to be. So I began to develop myself. I began investing in books, tapes, videos, then CD's, downloads and any other materials I could find that would help me develop as a God-fearing Christian man, with a purpose. It was a great endeavor, but I had no idea how tough of a task it would be.

Through the years, as I talk with men, I find a lack of awareness of life's timings or direction. Whenever they talk about what they want to do, there's never a sense of when or for how long. There's seldom a sense of aging, until we do age. Do we really know where we've been? Do we really know where we're going? Unless we learn to develop a realistic perspective of life, life will pass us by. Success is seldom achieved without deliberate planning and goal setting, and a lot of teamwork. The John Donne quotation that 'No man is an Island' stands so true.

It seems women are always aware of the stages of their lives. They've been preparing for it since before they hit puberty. They rally around each other, and they talk about it. They read countless magazine articles about it. There are countless books. There are the talk shows, the sitcoms, the dramas, and soaps. They have chat rooms and girls clubs, life groups and the infamous "Girls Night Out." I won't even mention the depth of the conversations that go on during those group bathroom visits! Men will never understand that one.

All the while, the men trudge along like a deer in headlights, not even thinking about what's next in life for them; from a physical sense, a mental sense and most importantly ... from a spiritual sense. Every stage of our life is important. If nothing else is accomplished through this book, I hope to make men aware that we don't live on earth forever! It is so important for us to be aware of where we are in our lives, and to have a definite working plan for each stage.

I thank God for my wife, Donna, who has encouraged me for years to write this book, so I can get out of me, what God has put in me. This is just a piece of my passion; to see men everywhere standing up and taking their rightful place as sons of God. We cannot help anyone or any situation if we are not the best "MAN" that we can be. If we don't know where we are going, how can we get there? If we don't know where we are going, how can we help someone else get there? We have too much at stake, to risk not carrying our load, and not leading the way.

Seldom do I find men that have taken a holistic view of their lives, or looked at their lives in stages or seasons. I find that not many men look at the stage of life which they have passed through, are passing through, or about to enter. If we are not looking from these different perspectives, we will never understand the discomfort we feel or the helplessness we feel of being in transition, from one stage to the next.

How can we be better fathers, sons, brothers, uncles, or friends if we don't understand who we are, or who we are supposed to be?

Our purpose is hidden in our journey.

By this I mean, any quest for substance in our life, will only be found in the process of fulfilling your purpose. I submit to you that no one knows you better than your creator Himself. If we do not have a relationship with God our Creator, how then can we know ourselves?

This book is a culmination of my experiences with teachers, ministries, retreats, studying, counseling, mentoring, working with, and being mentored by men. Don't think I didn't learn quite a bit from the women in my life, helping me to understand who I am! Through all of that, I consider this book to be a condensed view of men. It's not exhaustive or complete. It is simply some perspective to unfold or uncover some of the nuances that men may not be thinking about right now, but will face at some point in their lives, and even in the lives of others.

Being condensed is like that little capsule that comes out of the gumball machine, where you put it in a jar of water, and it becomes a larger foam dinosaur. Well, if you take the nuggets from this book, and put a little prayer and meditation on them, maybe it will become a larger foam dinosaur that will inspire you to dig deeper into a subject. It may lead to your taking the opportunity to discuss this writing with others. If that is so, then it will be the blessing I have prayed for it to be.

Read it. Enjoy it. As I was told many years ago, "eat the meat and spit out the bones." Don't be offended if I stepped on your toes. Don't be bitter. Choose to be better! In writing this from a place of authenticity and integrity, I had to take a few pot shots to the side myself, God reminded me of some of my own pitfalls. So don't think you're in this alone. It's not personal ... but yeah, it IS personal. As men, we have an obligation to fulfill God's purpose in our lifetime. When we do, we will help so many others along the way.

As you read through this material, recognize that these experiences are common, though not public, with many men. Over the years of stumbling, bumbling and falling on our faces, then finding ways of getting back up again, we endeavor to succeed in producing a life well lived. These experiences may not apply to every situation, but hopefully it will make you think more about your own life. Maybe it will give you a better perspective of your brothers, your friends, and your loved ones. My prayer is that it will inspire you to be more deliberate and proactive about your own precious life, the gift that God has given us.

~ Be Blessed,
Ellis C. McCarthy

ONE

THE CREATIVE DESIGNS OF THE MASTER BUILDER

In the beginning God created! The very first thing we read in the Bible about God is that He was working. In Genesis 1:1, before man was ever created, it says, "In the beginning God created the heaven and the earth." The message is the same in every language and every translation, God was working! He was working on building something great; something He conceived in His infinite wisdom. When He envisioned the idea to create, He developed a plan, just like a great craftsman or artist that wants to build a masterpiece—a signature project, the one piece of work by which he or she will be forever identified. Craftsmen sit down and think about what it is they want to build. I imagine God saying, "How about building a mini-me? A masterpiece that I can love and work with and adore—someone who can adore Me back, made in My Own image. I am *A love* love, *and I need* a living object to direct My love *That direct,* toward. I got it; let's make *man!*" And thus the adventure began, and the *blueprint* was created.

Ah, a blueprint! In *Merriam-Webster,* one of the definitions of *blueprint* is "something resembling a blueprint (as in serving as a model or providing

1

guidance); especially: a detailed plan or program of action [a blueprint for victory]." I love this particular definition, because it describes the one missing piece of that big puzzle we call *man,* and that is "a model for providing guidance." We're speaking my language now. If a builder needs a blueprint to build an inanimate object like a building, how much more do we men, who are living, breathing creatures, need a blueprint for our lives?

Whenever someone gets ready to draw a new design or blueprint, he or she already has a concept in mind. That person doesn't go to the drawing board with an empty mind and with no idea about what to create. Maybe that person doesn't have all the details of all the nooks and crannies of the project, but he or she pretty much has an idea about what to create. Although the drawing board may be blank at first, it gives endless possibilities to create whatever it is the designer has conceived. Sometimes in the process, the designer may get creative and add some new features, things that have been stirring around in their mind for a while. Maybe if that person is designing a building, he or she will think of something like automatic windows or remote entry systems—or how about adding a neat, new disposal system to the project?

I've worked in the information technology field, which they call IT today, for forty years. Imagine the number of changes and the creativity I've seen. When I started, they called it *data processing.* I've seen the name change many times over the years. I've been through *data processing, data management, computer services, information processing, business services, business technology, managed information systems,* and

2

information management, and the flavor for the day is *information technology.* We used to say in our business that the only thing that's constant is change. My job title has changed so many times that my family has a hard time telling people what I do for a living. I've seen so many advances in technology and it's moving so fast that I had to finally make the decision to get out of it. Well, the good Lord helped me with that decision. It's just so hard to keep up these days. I have so many "cloud services" that I get lost trying to figure out which planet the pictures from a family vacation are supposed to be on.

Let me go back a ways and give an example of some of the creative ideas that I've witnessed in my time. I worked in one building with an automated mail cart that rode around the floor delivering mail to all the secretary stations. It ran on magnetic tracks that were under the carpeting. It had rubber bumpers all around it, so if it got off the track and bumped into something, it would stop and do no damage. We called it Archie Bumper. Yeah, I know—for you old-timers, the name was a play on Archie Bunker, the lead character in the old *All in the Family* sitcom. Yeah, it's been that long!

Another example was when I worked in the Sears Tower when it was a pretty new building (since renamed Willis Tower—see what I mean?). It had a very unique window-washing system. Of all the thousands of tourists that visit that place every year, I wonder how many have ventured to ask, how in the world do they wash all those windows? We used to stand around and watch the automatic window-washing system. The building was so tall, 110 stories, the owners knew there was not enough money in all the world to pay somebody

3

to get up there and wash all those windows. Come on, think about it—this is Chicago, the Windy City!

All the windows were big floor-to-ceiling windows. Each section of the building had a schedule where the windows would get washed. It was quite amazing to see. I worked on the forty-seventh floor, where you could see some of the lower sections of the building getting their windows washed. The cleaning machine would come out its garage-like storage area, which was built into the top of each section of the building. It would roll out of its garage on tracks to the edge of the section and proceed down the side of the building. It would be attached to a track on the side of the building that you could not see. As the machine slid down the building, the lower opening of the machine would apply a water solution. The middle opening had rotating brushes that scrubbed the window, and the upper portion had a big squeegee that looked like a big double-bladed razor. It would rinse and remove the excess water from the window. Voilà! It's clean. It seemed that no matter how many times you saw this process, at some point in time, you found yourself staring out the window, looking at the windows getting washed.

I'm pretty sure the designer of that building wasn't considering the entertainment factor in what he created. Nor did he probably ever consider the countless man hours that would be spent gazing at his creation, especially while people were still on the clock! The point is that it served its purpose. Interesting point—before anything is designed, before any idea about creating something is conceived, even before a concept is approached, there is always a need.

4

They say that necessity is the mother of invention. When a need is recognized, the mind starts thinking of solutions to satisfy the need. Sometimes the solution involves things that exist, things that you can put your hands on, or things that you can acquire. Maybe adjustments or minor changes have to be made to something that exist to create the solution that fits the need. But sometimes there is no solution at all, and a solution has to be created.

When I think about the progress in technology over the last one hundred years, it's amazing how rapidly the world has advanced. It's so amazing, even to me, having worked in technology for forty years. As I was thinking about this, it dawned on me how amazing my God is. Think about it—He not only allowed the advancement in technology over the past one hundred years but created the whole earth in just six days! He created day and night, heaven and earth, the seas, the grass, the herb-yielding seed, the tree-yielding fruit, the greater light (the sun) and the lesser light (the moon), and the stars; He made birds, fish, cattle, creeping things, and beasts of the earth. Then after all of that, He turned around and made *man*! After His image and likeness, He created *man*!

God said, "Let us make Man in our image." He Himself was the prototype for the blueprint...He is God the Father, God the Son in the person of Jesus Christ, and God the Holy Spirit. Like Him we are three-part beings: spirit, soul, and body.

For what purpose did God make man? He had to have some need or some idea in his head before He made him; man would have to serve a purpose. A little later on, I'll talk about finding that purpose, even the individual purposes. We will examine ourselves and see if we can find the blueprints that God used in creating us.

Here is a passage in the Bible where David, who was the greatest king, is asking God the same questions we're asking today.

When I look at the night sky and see the work of your fingers—the moon and the stars you set in place. What are mere mortals that you should think about them, human beings that you should care for them? Yet you made them only a little lower than God and crowned them with glory and honor. You gave them charge of everything you made, putting all things under their authority—the flocks and the herds and all the wild animals, the birds in the sky, the fish in the sea, and everything that swims the ocean currents. O LORD, our Lord, your majestic name fills the earth! (Ps 8:3–6 NLT)

CREATIVE LEADERSHIP

"So God created man in his own image, in the image of God created he him; male and female created he them. And God blessed them, and God said unto them, be fruitful, and multiply, and replenish the earth, and subdue it: and have dominion over the fish of the sea, and over the fowl of the air, and over every living thing that move upon the earth" (Gn 1:27–28 NLT).

God expects real leadership from man. In the very first classroom, in life lesson number one, God told man to subdue the earth and have dominion over every living thing. When He gave this command to Adam, it appears that He gave it to just Adam, but He was also giving it to the preincarnate Eve (meaning before God took Eve from the side of Adam). She came out with everything God put into Adam and then some. Can I get an *amen* from the ladies!

When God was ready to proceed with turning the earth and its inhabitants over to man, He brought all the types of animals He created to Adam. He gave Adam the authority to give each animal its name. He listened to see what Adam would call each animal. In this one move, a number of things transpired. God had already given man the authority to name the animals when He commanded him to subdue and have dominion over the earth. He now expected Adam to exercise that authority. With authority always comes responsibility. No matter what that authority is, it comes with responsibility Remember that point when we make a decision or take action concerning our families. If you have the authority to make the decision, you have the responsibility for the results of that decision!

As a king sits on the throne, he gets all the adoration and accolades from his subjects. He gets boatloads of benefits just from being king. But a great king is only concerned about the well-being of his kingdom. He has the responsibility of the whole kingdom. It's the same way with our families. As kings in our homes, we have to be concerned with the well-being of our domains! If we don't provide for our domains, what kind of kings would we be? If the domains that we are kings over do not flourish, what kind of kings are we? If we do not develop our resources—meaning wives, children, homes, finances, health, or jobs—what would happen to the kingdom? If we do not build a support system of loving, nurturing, and truly caring for those we love, one day we'll find ourselves in need of the very support system that we were not able to build. Here's a new dynamic for you to think about. Build what you will need in your own future! You will have to be very creative to build a foundation to satisfy all the things you will need for the rest of your life.

Adam had so many animals to name; he had to be creative. God gives us the creativity and the provisions to produce what we need in our lives. Did Adam know that he was going to make a big mistake and need these animals to hide himself or that he was going to have to depend on these same animas to live, to eat, to provide shelter, to be a resource for his survival? I would say no, he didn't! But God did. He knew that Adam would have this need, so He allowed him—no, authorized him—to participate in creating or shaping what he would eventually need.

Notice what Adam called the animals is what the animals' names became. So the characteristics of a lion became what it means to be "lionish" or lionlike. The characteristics of a tiger became "tigerish." The characteristics of a bear became "bearish." Whatever they were had no identity; there was no way to describe them. Maybe up until that point they weren't even called "animals." He probably named them all "animals" as a group! When man exercised the authority that God gave him, those animals became lions and tigers and bears—oh, my! (OK, I couldn't help that one.)

So what are you naming? Is it an invention, a business, a song, or maybe that nameless something that has never been created? We all have needs in our lives, and many of us can easily recognize the needs in others' lives. Has it ever occurred to you that the ability to see the need just may be God prodding you to be creative and develop a solution?

God has given you the vision to see that thing that has not been described, that thing that has no identity or definition. To give it identity. To call it what *you* want to call it. The Bible says all things were created by Him and for Him (God, that is) (Co 1:16 KJV). It also says that there is no new thing under the sun (Ecc 1:9 KJV). That means God has created everything you need to build what God has placed in your vision. He's just waiting for you to name it, to give it definition. He wants you to identify it so that its existence, what God has already created in His mind, can be revealed by you!

Think about these inventions, where someone had to play the role of Adam. Now, for these inventions, we'll call them something like this:
- Car
- Computer
- Camera
- Internet
- Airplane
- Tweezers
- Bleach
- Paint
- Sewers
- Toilet and toilet paper (don't take it lightly; have you been on any good mission trips lately?)
- Roller coaster
- Embalming fluid (I bet that one made you think)

I've always said they could have had computers two thousand years ago. I know that sounds like a crazy idea, but it's true. What do we have now that they did not have two thousand years ago? Nothing. They even had electricity. Think about it. Where was electricity discovered? In lightning. There were a lot of things that had to be discovered, invented, created, learned, developed, and even conceived before computers could be invented. But it was all done with things that God had already provided in the earth. Were there any *new* substances that were created out of nothing that were used to create a computer? *No!* Over time, man has taken things God created and turned them into what we call "something new." But they were taken from "something old," and God allowed someone to be able to see the need and inspired him to be creative and find a way to meet that need.

I pray that God gives you the vision to see and the ears to hear the needs that are in the world so that you are able to find creative ways to take something old and create something new—something that meets the needs of God's people everywhere. And that He gets *all the glory* and praise for whatever it is that He allows you to create.

Thank God I Did It

Somebody said I couldn't do it.
They figured I would wait until I blew it.
I had no way to start today,
So I said, "I'll get around to it."

I was praying one day, asking God for His hand;
Didn't know all along He had a plan
That one day I'd rise to finish the prize.
By God, I think I can do it.

He took me in His hands and made a brand-new man.
Now I can do anything 'cause He willed me to it.
By God, I think I will do it!

Still no one believed what I could achieve.
I believed God said, "Go to it."
Now that I've heard and received His word,
By God, I've got to do it.

Now that it's done, everyone comes
Asking where in the world did I get it?
By praising God and taking a stand,
Thank God, He is able; I did it!

~ Ellis C. McCarthy ~

Two

HEART TO HEART

They say that first impressions stick. When people meet you for the very first time, what impression do they have of you when they walk away? Do they really have an impression of the real you? Do you give them an impression of someone you want to be or of something you want them to think? Can they really see you? Maybe they see the results of your life situation or your desires or failures or frailties. Or do they get an impression defined by someone else's perception of who you are?

Now ask yourself, what is God's impression of me? Moreover, what impression do you have of yourself? One of my favorite scriptures says,

> *"As in water face reflects face, so a man's heart reveals the man" (Prv 27:19 NKJV).*

This is to say that it doesn't matter what face you see in the reflection of the water or a mirror. What matters is what's in your heart. This is the real reflection of the man you're looking at in the water. This is a wake-up call, a call to do a self-evaluation of who you really are and what in the world you are doing with yourself. When you look in the mirror, what do you see? Does the impression you give reflect your heart, or does it reflect your face? This could be the face you put on this morning. This face could be affected by the circumstances you faced today. This face could be affected by your job, your wife, or your children. You could be saying, "This is just the face I want you to see right now." How many times do we give a false impression of who we really are? Just like in water, the face can be very much distorted from the truth. It is your heart that truly reflects who you really are.

How many times do we distort the truth of who we really are? How many people, if any, know the real you? How many know how your mind processes things? How much do you hold back concerning how you really feel about things? Doing this could actually be a very dangerous sign that something is wrong. When the mind of a man is left to his own thoughts, ways, and self-seeking satisfactions, he's not aware of the external entities that influence his thought process. He doesn't even realize the number of subliminal messages he's processing in his thoughts or who's driving them. Without being aware of these things, he's susceptible to the diabolical plots of the evil, self-satisfying minds of others: those in control of the national and international media and the massive amount of dollars spent on marketing to his mind-set. Take a second to think about what has influenced your decisions or the way you process them the most.

Unless you are very deliberate in every decision, those that you are not deliberate with usually are made based on the influence from someone else. So who's influencing those "nondecision" decisions? By that I mean the ones you don't even think about. Guess what, those decisions are a part of who we are. They also reflect what's in our hearts.

As I mentioned before, we are a three-*part* being: spirit, soul, and body. The body was made from the dust of the ground. The spirit was breathed into us directly from God himself. We can't see it, but it is the thing that makes us an individual person. Then there is the soul.

In his teaching "The Soul of a Man," Bishop Tudor Bismark teaches about the components of the soul, which are the will, the emotions, and the heart. His teaching enlightened me and gave me an understanding of a number of issues I've dealt with in my life. I would suggest everyone get a copy of that teaching and study it and determine the benefits you can gain from this knowledge for yourselves.

In his teaching, Bishop Bismark says the will is the mind; it is a compilation of thoughts and ideas or the ability to make decisions and choices. The emotions are the "feelings" part of a person—things that make you feel a certain way, like good food and good music. Other things, like fragrance or environments, can make you feel good or make you feel bad. Many times we make judgments or act on our emotions.

Then there is the *heart*. The heart is your intent. It determines the character or structure of your thinking. It is a place that determines things like arrogance, characteristics, or traits of behavior. It is also your consciousness and your awareness of who you are.

14

I reference this because Proverbs 27:19 deals with the fact that it is what's in the internal workings of the heart that reveals who we really are ("so a man's heart reveals the man").

Most of man's issues of life are formulated out of the intent of the heart. This is where your characteristics and traits of behavior are determined. The intent influences the way we think and the way we feel. As I ponder the driving force behind our intentions, the word *creed* comes to mind. Your creed is normally associated with a statement of religion, but it also identifies your belief system. The decisions you make and the things you intend to do are based on what your belief system says is the right thing for you to do.

Most of the issues we have in life are because of decisions we've made or decisions others have made for us, which we've accepted. "Keep thy heart with all diligence; for out of it are the issues of life" (Prv 4:23).

In the heart is where wickedness begins to take shape. The mind takes the intent and starts planning the intended outcome. Then, speaking and acting on it produces the wickedness of the heart. "The heart is deceitful above all things, and desperately wicked: who can know it?" (Jer 17:9 KJV).

I would include our passions as a matter of the heart. Your passion also drives your intent. Every man should be passionate about something! We have to ask ourselves, what is the source of our passion? Is this something God has placed in us, or is it something we are just lusting after? Ask yourself, does that thing you want or are going after only benefit yourself? You selfishly consider that the thing will make you look better or feel better. But when you find your divine passion, it will benefit many. Your thought process will not take into consideration the benefits to yourself.

7 What a man is passionate for, he will pursue. Men are usually talking about and acting on what they are pursuing. When men are pursuing their divine passions, it's because those passions are deep in their hearts. That's when we have a different persona about ourselves, and we have our game face on. We're more confident and have a sense of purpose. This in itself will change the impressions that we give. People will be able to see it. There will always be a good report about the person you are. Your passion exudes from your heart. It motivates you to get up and do something. It gives you that extra boost of energy, even when you don't have any. It becomes your number one pursuit.

Right now I'm pursuing my divine passion. It's to share my experience, wisdom, and knowledge with you. It's what's driving me right now. My prayer is that there is something here that you can use to benefit your family, church, community, and most of all yourself! I know that God has given me this information for your benefit. I know He gave it to me, because I could not come up with this myself. And I have witnessed this information be a blessing to many men. I get great pleasure in knowing that people are blessed by what God has given to us.

I'm also writing this for my sons, daughters, grandchildren, and beyond. I pray the benefit of this writing will go far beyond my own life. I was moved by the fact that Abraham was chosen as the father of faith.

Enoch pleased God to the point that he just walked into heaven. Noah preached about rain for 120 years and built an ark at a time when there was probably no such thing as a flood. Why, then, was Abraham chosen above these guys? Genesis 18:19 says, "For I know him, that he will command his children and his household after him, and they shall keep the way of the LORD, to do justice and judgment; that the LORD may bring upon Abraham that which he hath spoken of him" (KJV).

My passion is that I want to teach my children to keep the way of the Lord and do justice and judgment!

So the question is, what are you passionate about, and what are you pursuing? Is it something that you are lusting after for your own pleasure, or is it something deep down inside of you that's for the benefit of others?

Better yet, I should be able to look at what you are pursuing and see what you are passionate about!

Let your actions speak louder than your words. And let your words produce what's reflected in your heart. That's when your heart will reflect the real you. Now, are the impressions we give going to be based on our faces or on our hearts? What impressions are you giving?

Selah! (That means pause here, take a minute, and think about it!)

MY WORD IS MY BOND

Why is it so important to be honest and truthful? Has anyone ever told you that the power of life and death is in your tongue? That means not only the length of your life, but also the quality of your life. Your mouth is directly tied to your heart. The mouth will speak what fills the heart. "A good man brings good things out of the good stored up in his heart, and an evil man brings evil things out of the evil stored up in his heart. For the mouth speaks what the heart is full of" (Lk 6:45 NIV).

Here is another translation of that verse from another biblical writer: "For whatever is in your heart determines what you say. A good person produces good things from the treasury of a good heart, and an evil person produces evil things from the treasury of an evil heart" (Mt 12:35 NLT).

The heart is judged by what comes out of your mouth. In between your mouth and your actions is the intent of your heart. Your mouth will speak and produce based on the intent of your heart. If your heart is not good and the intent is selfish and evil, the mouth produces lies and deception. If your heart is good and your intent is good, your mouth will produce truth from the goodness of your heart. Your mouth will produce truths or lies, depending on the intent of your heart.

Whether we know it or not, we are judged every time we open our mouths. You know the old saying "my word is my bond." Your integrity and credibility is determined by the accuracy of what you say. That includes doing what you say you will do and saying the state of things as you see them. An example of the state of things could be as simple as this: if you said it is cold outside, and I put on a heavy jacket and go outside but find it to be warm, what would I think about what you said? Are you nuts? It's nice out here!

Or what if I said I just found out from a fantastic inside source that company A was going to buy company B next week, and the stock was going to skyrocket. Then next week came, and it was company B that actually bought company A, and the stock was devalued and dropped considerably. What would you think about my next stock tip? What if you found out that I secretly dumped all my stock in companies A and B and bought company C's stock, which benefited from the merger of companies A and B. Now what do you think of me?

Another way our integrity and credibility is judged is if we do what we say we will do. If I say I will call you tonight, and two days later I see you, what is the first thing that comes to your mind? "Hey, you were supposed to call me." What if I tell my wife I'll get off work at 4:00 p.m. and be there to pick her up at 4:30 p.m., and it's 6:15 p.m. before I get there? Why do you think she's sitting somewhere with what my dad called "rocks in her jaws?" What do you think is going to happen when I do get there to pick her up? Do you really expect her to welcome me with open arms? It'll be more like World War III. Boy, you wouldn't want to be in my shoes at that point. Been there, done that, won't do it anymore! What do you think she is going to say when I tell her the next day that I'll pick her up at 4:30 p.m.? Get the picture?

This is the same in business, family, church, friendships, and even with yourself. Sometimes we can't even be true to ourselves. We used to call it "writing a check that your butt can't cash!" When we make promises that we hope, believe, or desire to keep, somehow, even though we think we can or try, we often fail. Why is that? Do our tongues line up with our abilities? Did you ever hear the quote from Shakespeare's *Hamlet,* "To thine own self be true?" The following lines contain a statement explaining that your truth must be at the same level of consistency as the day following the night and therefore cannot be untrue to any man; not even yourself.

There is a verse in the Bible that says it is better not to vow than to vow and not pay. Why? Because there's more value in our integrity than our promise. There's more credibility in what we *do* than what we *say.* There's more to lose by not doing what we say than there is to not say or promise anything at all.

Some people will tell lies to try to make people believe what they want them to believe about themselves to gain credibility with others. Often the very person they are trying to impress can see right through them. If they don't already have a history with that person, they just began one; a bad one, I might add. So if the person they're trying to impress can't see it now, the track record will eventually catch up to them, and before you know it, the credibility is gone.

My oldest daughter wanted to give me a birthday present but couldn't afford it, so she wrote me a blank check for my birthday. I said, "Oh, wow!" When I looked at the signature line, it was signed, "Jesus Paid It All!" Instantly, there went her credibility, out the window. My first thought was, "Don't ever, ever, *ever,* and never take another check from her again! Any kind." Thank God He has delivered her into a prosperous career. Now I'm taking that check back to her and cashing it in. Hmm, now let's see here, how much do I want to write it for?

Even when you sign for credit, it's based on your FICO score. What does the FICO score tell about you? It measures the likelihood of whether you will keep your promise to pay your debt. It tells your creditworthiness. The FICO score, originally introduced in 1989, takes into account various factors in your credit history to determine the level of risk of default in lending you money. If you sign up for credit and never intend to pay it or always pay it late, isn't that a lie? That's where the FICO score comes in to tell on you. Here is where the intent is separating the mouth and the heart. You knew you couldn't afford that thing when you bought it. Where is the integrity; where is the credibility?

Some people live most of their lives with lies hanging over their heads. They are bound by the fear of being exposed. Only the truth can free you from that bondage. When we talk about the heart revealing the man, it is the truth in his heart and his mouth that will build trust and credibility. It is the integrity of his heart that will measure the man.

> "Trust is the glue of life. It's the most essential ingredient in effective communication. It's the foundational principle that holds all relationships."
>
> ~ Steven Covey

I hope that after reading this chapter, you can use your will to make the decision to set your intent on truth and honesty—truth and honesty with yourself and everyone with whom you interact. You will be relieved of the burden of any lies that may be hanging over your head. You will become more concerned with the truth than any gain from the lie. When your divine passion is pursued in truth and integrity, you will grow in your pursuit, because good things will come out of a good heart. This will increase your ability, opportunities, and results. It stops the roadblocks. I'm not saying it will be easy or without opposition. But it will keep you on the correct path of your divine purpose, a purpose that will make a difference in the lives of many people.

So if you ever been less than truthful, say something like this:

"God, I realize I haven't always been true to myself and others or to You. Forgive me, and keep me on a path of truth and righteousness. Amen."

"The Measure Of A Man"

Not—How did he die? But—How did he live?
Not—What did he gain? But—What did he give?

These are the things that measure the worth
Of a man as a man, regardless of birth.

Not—What was his station? But—had he a heart?
And—How did he play his God-given part?

Was he ever ready with a word of good cheer?
To bring back a smile, to banish a tear?

Not—What was his church?
Not—What was his creed?
But—Had he befriended those really in need?

Not—What did the sketch in the newspaper say?
But—How many were sorry when he passed away?

These are the things that measure the worth
Of a man as a man, regardless of birth.

~ Anonymous ~

-Three-

ON PURPOSE

Every time God speaks, there is opportunity—an opportunity to make a good decision. When this opportunity comes, we have an opportunity for obedience (good) or an opportunity for disobedience (evil). These choices determine our destinies.

> *"Do what is good and run from evil so that you may live!" (Am 5:14 NLT)*

When I was a boy, my brothers and I were, as described by my dad, "a little hardheaded." We would be in the house tossing around some kind of a ball, and Pop, as we called him, would come in and say, "Cut it out, no playing ball in the house," and we would stop. But of course as soon as he left, we would start tossing the ball around again. Before you know it, we would break a window or lamp. He would hear it and come back in and say, "Boy, why did you do that—you did that on purpose." Wow, here it comes.

DISOBEDIENCE

One thing about disobedience: it always carries baggage. I call this baggage *ramifications* and *consequences*.

They cannot be avoided. Once you've chosen to disobey, they are on the clock. You do not get to choose these ramifications or consequences; they always choose you. You also have no choice when this baggage will come. In other words, once you disobey, you have no idea what the ramifications or consequences will be.

When we disobeyed, we didn't understand why my dad said, "You did that on purpose!" We thought he was saying that we deliberately broke the glass, since he asked, "Why did you do that?"

He was really asking, "Why did you decide to continue throwing the ball?" By continuing to do what we were told not to, we knowingly accepted the consequences and ramifications of our decision. And now...we've got the baggage! We've got the ramifications and consequences, which become the purpose of disobedience. The job of disobedience is always to distract and separate us from our purposes.

Sometimes those consequences and ramifications pile up on you. Have you ever heard the saying, "Your past will catch up with you?" This saying might as well read, "The ramifications and consequences are going to catch up to you." Well, sometimes my brothers and I would think we'd gotten away with something, especially when it was something we thought was really small or insignificant. My dad would find out about it and let us off the hook at that time. But he would cap it with, "You better look out, because when I get you, I'm gonna get you for old and new." The next time we did something—again, something that we thought was insignificant—here comes the ramifications and consequences. Sometimes I think, what if we had lived in today's world, where you can't beat your kids silly? Because for what he gave us, we would have been going to see Pop on visitation days. Don't get me wrong, he never would injure any of us, but he sure believed the scriptures about how to handle your kids, that's for sure. He sure didn't spare the rod. Guess what—thank God, it worked! Because of the discipline and obedience he demanded from us, it saved our lives!

When we recognize ourselves being disobedient, our tendency is to run from God. We try to hide it, make the best of it, rationalize it, even sometimes admit it and call it a mistake. What we're doing is trying to avert or minimize the ramifications and consequences. Guess what? God knows it all. Even if we delay it, it's coming.

In the Bible, Adam and Eve ate the fruit off the forbidden tree—oh, you know the story. What happened next? They hid. When God was looking for them in one place, they were someplace else in the garden. God asked Adam, "Where art thou?" When He asked this question, it's not because He didn't know where Adam was. Remember, He spoke right to him. When God asks you a question, it's not because He doesn't know the answer, it's because He's trying to get you to recognize the real answer. Maybe Adam should have thought a little more about eating that fruit before he even had to answer for it. Disobedience caused him to have a four-part answer. He said "I heard you walking in the garden, so I hid. I was afraid because I was naked." (Gen 3:10 NKJV) Let's look at what happened and what he was saying:

- "I heard your voice." God's voice brought fear of discovery, fear of authority; there's no evidence Adam had ever been afraid of God before.

- "I hid." This is temporary avoidance of a sure penalty.
- "I was afraid." Fear of the ramifications and consequences entered Adam.
- "I was naked." Adam is saying, "I'm vulnerable." Shame entered his heart and changed his normal actions.

No matter what Adam thought he was trying to do, it had an effect on every generation. We are all still feeling the ramifications and consequences! You need to read the story in the book of Genesis. When God said, "Who told you that you were naked?" Adam did the man thing. He blamed the woman. He said, "It was the woman you gave me who gave me the fruit, and I ate it" (Gen 3:12 NKJV). Of course, as usual, God did not take that for an excuse. Men have been suffering the consequences and ramifications ever since.

Have you ever heard that obedience is better than sacrifice? This is true when you take the very thing that you have been given explicit instructions about, disobey those instructions, and then expect good to come from doing whatever it is *you* want to do. At some point you made the decision that satisfying your own desires—or the desires of others—superseded the instructions. This is actually saying that your desires not only supersede the instructions, but they actually supersede the One in authority who gave the instructions. This is where your will comes into agreement with the purpose of disobedience.

There is a Bible story where God sent a message to a king and told him to go and destroy a city and everything in it. The king did destroy it, but he kept the best

27

animals and beasts so he could use them for their own sacrifices to God. That's when the king was told it is better to obey than to sacrifice. Because of that, that king lost his kingdom and his life.

Now, what are you sacrificing in order to do your own thing? When we are disobedient, sometimes we don't realize what we are sacrificing. When we get that feeling that tells us we're supposed to be doing something, or we actually get instructions and we choose to ignore them, there will be a sacrifice. We are sacrificing the intended results of our obedience.

OBEDIENCE

> *"Therefore we ought to give the more earnest heed to the things which we have heard, lest at any time we should let them slip" (Heb 2:1–2 KJV).*

Obedience doesn't have baggage; it has benefits. These benefits are the results of your obedience placing you in the will of God for your life, also known as divine purpose. If you are going to obey God, you have to be able to hear His voice and receive His instructions.

There is a passage in the Bible that speaks of hearing the voice of God. It speaks of God as a shepherd and us as his sheep. "When he has brought out all his own, he goes before them, and the sheep follow him, for they know his voice. A stranger they will not follow, but they will flee from him, for they do not know the voice of strangers" (Jn 10:4–5 ESV).

Although this is a metaphorical story, it is very true. When you learn the voice of God, you really will be hungry to follow Him. When my wife and I were on a mission trip in Israel, we were touring a site known as Beit She'an. This is the place in the Bible where they hung the bodies of Israel's first king, Saul, and his three sons. While we were there, a shepherd came through the site with a herd of sheep, which seemed to be about a hundred sheep or more. He would whistle and call "boy, boy, boy" as he led them. As the sheep passed us, we tried to imitate the shepherd to see if we could redirect the sheep. Forget about it! Not happening. The shepherd stopped by us and allowed us to see the sheep and pet the sheepdog while the sheep were watering. But when he began to whistle and say "boy, boy," the sheep stopped whatever they were doing and followed that shepherd. We could not distract those sheep from drinking or grazing or just standing around. Nor could we keep them from following their shepherd.

We need to be just like those sheep. Get in tune with God's voice, and obey unconditionally. We shouldn't let anything distract us from where He is leading us.

God speaks to us in many ways. It's rare for him to speak audibly. But He gives what some of the older generation call an *unction*. That's a deep-down feeling that won't leave you alone. Sometimes it will come from a man or woman of God that He's using to speak to you. There are other ways also. But however His voice comes, it comes in peace. If you are a child of God, you will learn His voice. And when He speaks, His words are always going to be in line with His purpose for you.

When you are a child of God and obedient to the voice of God, you are deeply imbedded in His purpose. How do I know? Because the word of God tells me,

> *"And we know that all things work together for good to them that love God, to them who are the called according to his purpose" (Rom 8:28 NLT).*

Most men don't understand what their purpose is, and most of them get lost in the pursuit of trying to find it.

I can see how finding our purpose becomes our number one pursuit. But I think we have it backward. Instead of being in the pursuit of purpose, we ought to be in pursuit of God.

> *"But seek ye first the kingdom of God, and his righteousness; and all these things shall be added unto you" (Mt 6:33 NLT).*

If you seek God, you will find Him! The more you pursue God, the clearer your purpose becomes. The Bible describes David, the king of Israel, as "a man after God's own heart." (Act 13:22 KJV) I'm not sure why, but I always looked at this statement as though God was so enamored with David that He kept David on His heart. But taking a different perspective of the statement, I see that it was David that was always in pursuit of God. In other words, he was the one "going after God." I would say he definitely found his divine purpose and fulfilled the will of God for his life.

David took advantage of the opportunities God put before him. When opportunity knocks, we have to hear God first. Then there is a decision to make. Disobey and get the "baggage," or obey and operate according to purpose, on *His* purpose. If you want to see the potential unlocked in your life, obedience is the key. Obedience to God will always lead you to your purpose.

Only in God will we find our true divine purpose. So when you hear that knock, when you answer it, you must be deliberate, and you must do it **on purpose!**

OBEDIENCE will Always lead you to your purpose.

OBecher the Key Amen

-Four-
THE BUILDING

As we move from the pursuit of purpose to the pursuit of God and our purpose in Him, let's look at how we can formulate our hearts' intent to pursue God first.

We get to a point in our lives where we ask ourselves the questions, why did God make me, or why did God create mankind? Let's examine some things that we know. At some point, God had to have what I call the "Blueprint of a God Man'."

The Bible says that when God created man, He created him in His own image and likeness. But I must question, is that how we see ourselves? Our view of ourselves is often distorted. As a matter of fact, our view of ourselves is always distorted. We don't always see ourselves as spirit, soul, and body. We view ourselves through our earth consciousness. That means we view ourselves as a product of our heredity, our environment, our education, our finances, our family, our past, and even our future. Those things make up and shape our personalities.

Although we are made in God's image and likeness,

when I try to picture God, I don't see myself. Neither I do I see all those things I listed that make up my personality. The next question is, when someone else looks at me, do they see God? Then who are we really? Well, I learned it like this. I am a person made in the image of God, and I am a spirit, I have a soul, and I live in a body. I once heard a great preacher say that He made us this way so that with the body, we become earth conscious; with the soul, we become self-conscious, and with the spirit, we become God conscious. Selah!

[handwritten margin notes: Body / Earth / Soul/self / conscious / Spirit/God / conscious]

Our distorted view of ourselves reminds me of the story in the Bible where a man names Nicodemus came to Jesus to ask a question, and Jesus told him, "you must be born again" (Jn 3:7 NLT). So I thought about the next question that Nicodemus asked Jesus: "How can an old man go back into his mother's womb and be born again?" (Jn 3:4 NLT) Oh, that was a tease; you gotta go read the rest of the story to get the answer to that.

A few days ago, I was in the barbershop, and my barber, Mike, was telling me a story about an encounter that he had with an old friend. Mike had been pondering that age-old question that men usually come to: What the heck is going on in my life? And during his story, I was impressed to tell him about the new building analogy.

Mike began to tell me about the conversation with this old friend, and this is how his conversation went. Mike said to me, "Man, God has really been dealing with me. He's got me reading my Bible every day. And you know how it seems like when you're looking for a word from God, but can never get it? It's like you'll be sitting in church, and there's a prophet in the church, and they seem to go to everybody but you. Then just when you think they are coming your way, they go to the person standing right behind you." Then Mike continued, "So anyway, I was at this bar"—of course my mind goes, OK, Mike, how did we jump from church to the bar?— "You know, I saw this old friend of mine, and he began to tell me about all the good things that had been happening to him.

He went on about how he gave his life to Christ and all the things that transpired since then. He told me about myself and that I didn't recognize how much God has helped me. How I had some old buildings that were driving my finances in a hole. And he told me how I had multiple girlfriends with all this 'baby momma drama.' And how I seemed to have no direction, and then all of a sudden I started making good decisions. He pointed out how I seemed to get myself out of all the mess I was in. And now I'm single, not dating, out of bankruptcy, have an apartment, and have good credit." This friend said to Mike, "Man, that's just God working in your life." He told Mike to read the thirty-one books of Proverbs in the Bible. He said to read one book every day and watch what God does. Mike then told me, "As my friend was talking to me, it was like out of the blue, God was saying to me, 'Here's that word you were looking for.'" As I listened to Mike tell this story, that's when it came to me to tell Mike about the new building analogy; here it is.

A number of years ago, I was working with a guy who joined the church where we attended. He was struggling with his family. He was not married, but he lived with a woman, and they had a few teenage children, plus a few nieces and nephews that also lived with them. This guy really struggled being successful at anything. He could never find his place. He really needed what I call a perspective adjustment. At first he would not come to church at all. After a while, he would come to church periodically and bring his pseudofamily. He would come to men's events and participate in any special services, but he still struggled in his everyday life. I was talking to him one day, and I heard the Lord say, "He is an incomplete building." God had a plan for his life that could not be completed because he was not complete as a man.

As I began talking to him, I kind of had no idea what I was saying at the time, but God told me to use the analogy of tearing down a building or a house and building a new one. This analogy would show him how God tears down a man and builds a completely new one in us. Sometimes we feel like we have to be perfect in order for God to use us. I hear people say, "I'm not ready to join church or become a Christian because I have a number of areas in my life I need to get together before I can do that." But there are plenty of examples in the Bible where God uses imperfect people to execute His perfect will. I was actually one of those imperfect people, with my own issues, speaking to that struggling man that day. God receives us just like we are right now, imperfections and all. In the process of fulfilling God's purpose, He is constantly working on completing our buildings.

God gave me the analogy of a man being like a new building or house replacing an old, vacant building. Even though this is just a metaphor, it has some interesting symmetry with the process of building a man. When a new building is needed on a property and an old building is standing there, the first thing that has to happen is that the old building has to come down!

When we are living in our sinful natures and don't know Jesus as our Lord and savior, we are like an old, broken-down building that needs to be demolished and rebuilt—just like when Jesus said to Nicodemus, "You must be born again." (Jn 3:7 NLT) He's saying that you must be rebuilt as a man, as God intended in His original design for your life, according to His blueprint. Here comes the wrecking ball to tear down the old building. This is when you begin to recognize that what you are doing is not working for you, and things are beginning to crumble in your life.

No matter how hard you fight and try to stand your ground, the wrecking ball is swinging your way. A good measure of this wrecking ball coming is by what you may be thinking about at night before you go to bed or what you may be thinking about when you wake up in the morning. If at either of those times you're saying to yourself, "Man, this isn't working. I've gotta get something going for myself" or "man, it seems like no matter how good things look around me, something is missing"—this is an indication that the wrecking ball is coming your way and that God wants to rebuild you and give you a solid foundation on which to stand. As things seem to get tougher internally or things begin to fall, although we are determined to fight, sometimes we just give up. Usually that means throwing in the towel and just letting whatever happens happen or reluctantly admitting we need help. This is a prime point for us to have someone close to us that can say, "Man, been there, done that!"

Recognize where you are in life. It's like recognizing and accepting the fact that the wrecking ball is coming and that you need it. When the wrecking ball strikes and it seems like your world has crumbled, then the bulldozers are coming behind it to sweep away the rubble left over from the damage of the wrecking ball. Then comes the excavation! *Excavation* means to dig a hole. I don't mean the hole we seem to have dug for ourselves. I'm talking about the hole that God is digging in our hearts. Another Marriam Webster definition for the word *excavate* is to expose by digging. What God is doing when this hole is dug is *exposing our dirt and getting the dirt out!* I call this the "bulldozer of repentance."

Repentance, or to repent, means acknowledging that you need a change and choosing to change. It means choosing to let go of the past and all the wrong thinking and all the things produced from a bad heart. It means looking to be forgiven for all the wrong that ever occurred in your life. Repentance will get the dirt out of our lives.

When we repent, we feel like a bulldozer has come and lifted piles of rubble and boulders off our shoulders. But to finish the job, we have to acknowledge the One who's driving that bulldozer, lifting the rubble, and freeing us. His name is Jesus. What you're feeling is Jesus standing before us with His arms open, saying, "If you confess with your mouth that Jesus is Lord and believe in your heart that God raised him from the dead, you will be saved." (Rom 10:9 NLT)

If you have never done that, *right now* is a very good place to start that rebuilding process—yes, right now.

Even if the wrecking ball and bulldozers have not come into your life, I'm sure that if you truly examine yourself, you'll see the markings of a crumbling building or maybe even recognize that your struggles are steering the course. Even when we feel like we have it all together, there's always that something that's missing that keeps us from experiencing real peace. I'm not talking about the false sense of hope that says "I can do this." I'm talking about real inner peace.

Even if you have a different belief system and don't believe the things you've heard about Jesus, what if you're wrong? Have you ever wondered if there is a way to prove it, one way or another? Then try this. Ask Jesus, the bulldozer driver Himself, to come and show Himself to you or prove His existence. I believe that if you ask Him, He will do it.

If you have no apprehension and want that change in your life, just read this out loud:

"I confess that Jesus is Lord, and I believe in my heart that God raised Him from the dead. Lord, forgive me for my sins, give me a clean heart, and make me a new man, and *I am saved!*"

It's that simple. *Belief*

Romans 10:10–13 says, "For it is by believing in your heart that you are made right with God, and it is by confessing with your mouth that you are saved. As the Scriptures tell us, 'Anyone who trusts in him will never be disgraced.' Jew and Gentile are the same in this respect. They have the same Lord, who gives generously to all who call on him. For 'everyone who calls on the name of the Lord will be saved.'"

The new building process has begun! Let's just pause here to give God some praise for what He has just done in your life! Hallelujah!

Having salvation is not the end of the process—it's the beginning. It starts the journey to finding and fulfilling God's divine purpose for your life. And to say the least, quite a journey it will be!

FINISHING THE BUILDING
Let me continue with the analogy God gave me and continue to look at that blueprint to see the symmetry between the house being built and man.

When Nicodemus, a ruler of the Jews, snuck in one night to speak to Jesus, he had an inkling that this Jesus was someone special, acknowledging that He was sent by God. And when Jesus said to him, "Except a man be born again, he cannot see the kingdom of God," (Jn 3:3 KJV) Jesus was saying that you cannot get to heaven without being rebuilt as a house of God.

Once the excavation is complete and all the dirt is out (praise God), the foundation is poured. In Mat 16:13-16, Jesus once asked the disciples, "Who do men say that I, the Son of Man, am?" Peter answered and said "You are the Christ, the Son of the living God." Jesus then told Peter he was blessed because man did not tell him that Jesus was the Messiah, but God himself did. And this revelation of who Jesus was would be the rock, or foundation, on which His church would be built. And that includes you! This is the foundation that we stand on, with Jesus as the cornerstone that holds it all together. A little later we'll talk about other foundations in our lives.

Whenever you pour a new foundation, it has to cure. Then it's tested. The testing of the foundation starts when there's what you call a *backfill*. A backfill is when the bulldozer returns and brings the dirt back *against*—I repeat, *against*—the foundation to surround it as it settles into place. This puts the foundation under pressure. This pressure will test the foundation to see if it can withstand the pressure of the dirt or whether it moves or cracks under pressure. This pressure is when Satan brings back all the dirt that you were involved with to test you to see if your foundation will crack. To see if you'll go back to the lifestyle or sin you once had and depended on. Or will you stand cured on the revelation of who Jesus is in your life?

Even if we crack a little, don't give in, don't feel bad. You have to remember that bulldozer driver. He's the one in control. He's always there to forgive and restore. Remember, He is the one actually pushing the dirt around, and He knows that you have the capacity to withstand any dirt trying to come back in your life! And know that this is just the beginning!

> *"Dear brothers and sisters, when troubles come your way, consider it an opportunity for great joy. For you know that when your faith is tested, your endurance has a chance to grow. So let it grow, for when your endurance is fully developed, you will be perfect and complete, needing nothing"* (Jas 1:2–4 NLT).

I love the King James Version of this scripture. It says,

"Count it all joy when ye fall into divers temptations."
In other words, rejoice in this testing because it not
only gives opportunity to test the foundation, but it also
gives us the assurance that this foundation can be
perfect for building on.

If this foundation does not break up under pressure,
then it is ready to be built upon. When God built
(created) man, he was just a lump of dirt. But God had
a blueprint in mind of what He wanted this lump of
clay to become.

I like to imagine God working from a blueprint, just
like a house being built on a solid foundation. And just
like a house, He puts us together piece by piece.

He starts by building the framework of the house,
which is like our skeletal and muscular systems—our
bones, joints, ligaments, and muscles.

Then he adds our electrical works, which is our
neurological system—the brain and wiring of our
nervous systems, so we can have impulses, alarms,
lighting, and communication systems that work. This is
including our five senses: taste, touch, smell, hearing,
and sight.

Then comes the plumbing and sewage piping, which is
our gastrointestinal or digestive system.

He puts in the heating and air conditioning units, which
are like our respiratory systems so we can breathe and
sweat glands to cool us off.

And finally our layers of brick, siding, drywall, and

carpet for our integumentary system—our skin, our hair, our nails, and a fresh coat of paint for our complexions.

And after all of this is done, we are still just a lump of clay. And we still need a cardiovascular system, because we still don't have a heart or blood pumping through our veins. I remember a secular singer named Luther Vandross who passed away a few years ago. He recorded a song he made famous called "A House is not a Home." The song says "a house is not a home, if there's no one living there." The wonderful thing that God did was to breathe Himself in us. The Bible says, "And man became a living soul!" (Gen 2:7 KJV) Now take a really deep breath, and feel God in you! He breathed His Own Spirit into us to occupy the house that He built. That's when the house became our home. The Bible calls it "an house not made with hands." (2 Co 5:1 KJV)

THE COMPLETE MAN

Here's how I use the building analogy in relation to the complete man. Each part of the building should relate to its function for the whole man, including the spiritual man and the soul, not just the body.

For example, our frame-up, or skeletal system, represents the structure of life that you've established—the foundations you've built and the things that stand on your foundation. These are the day-to-day activities and decisions or the way you go about achieving your goals, things that affect your productivity and your accomplishments, or things you've accumulated over time that contribute to your lifestyle and well-being.

Next is the electrical system, which is your neurological or nervous system. The body has electricity in it to regulate your heartbeat and brain function. Your body is like a computer or a transformer; it has a certain capacity it can contain and handle. But in God's man, the electrical system represents your spirit, which connects with God. It is also the conductor of the anointing. Just like the body has a capacity for electricity, you have a capacity for the anointing, which is the power of God in you. An overload of electricity will electrocute your body. Unlike the capacity of the body, there is no limit or overload of the anointing of God.

The plumbing or digestive system is to take in the necessary nutrients for living and to filter out all the unnecessary junk. This compares with walking in truth or not living a lie or in deception. You take in or process truth, and the lies or hidden things will be exposed, and destructive things will be weeded out. The truth will always prevail, and so will you.

Our heating and air conditioning is the respiratory system used to breathe in what God has given us. The respiratory system relates to us stopping and thinking about Him breathing into us and giving us all that we have. It's a place to meditate on His goodness toward us and to truly worship God. It's a point of rest and relaxation and restoration.

The integumentary system is the skin or outer coat that protects the body from various kinds of damage. The brick and siding are the outer shell of the body and the face you reflect. You should be reflecting the stage of life where you truly are, right now. So many times we want to reflect an image that doesn't tell the true story.

And we wonder sometimes why people misjudge who we are. We should be reflecting the person or building that God built, which is *your* revelation of God and His word. This where we have to wake up every morning prepared to put on the whole armor of God.

> *A final word: Be strong in the Lord and in his mighty power. Put on all of God's armor so that you will be able to stand firm against all strategies of the devil. For we are not fighting against flesh-and-blood enemies, but against evil rulers and authorities of the unseen world, against mighty powers in this dark world, and against evil spirits in the heavenly places. Therefore, put on every piece of God's armor so you will be able to resist the enemy in the time of evil. Then after the battle you will still be standing firm. Stand your ground, putting on the belt of truth and the body armor of God's righteousness. For shoes, put on the peace that comes from the Good News so that you will be fully prepared. In addition to all of these, hold up the shield of faith to stop the fiery arrows of the devil. Put on salvation as your helmet, and take the sword of the Spirit, which is the word of God. Pray in the Spirit at all times and on every occasion. Stay alert and be persistent in your prayers for all believers everywhere. (Eph 6:10–18 NLT)*

You have been constructed in His likeness and in the image of God. My hope is that you declare, as I and many others like you have, that "as for me and my house, we shall serve the Lord!" (Jos 24:15 KJV)

> *"Unless the LORD builds the house, the builders labor in vain. Unless the LORD watches over the city, the guards stand watch in vain" (Ps 127:1).*

-Five-

FOUNDATIONS

In the last chapter, I used some creative liberties to give a fun kind of view of a man as a building. But this chapter gets a little more serious with looking at foundations. We've established that the foundation of the church is the revelation of who Jesus is. It is He who has built the church on that foundation. But as a man, what foundation do you stand on? There's a scripture that asks the question, "If the foundation be destroyed, what shall the righteous do?" (Ps 11:3). This verse really made me think about the foundations we depend on today, such as our government, our economy, and our jobs. We need these things in place just to survive every day. And it seems they are always on the verge of being destroyed or broken down. So we have to ask ourselves, can we survive a breakdown of the systems of the world?

Whatever your foundation is, it had better be sure, strong, and solid. When we talk about laying any foundation, it has to sit on something that can bear the weight of that foundation; it also has to be balanced in order to distribute the weight of whatever it has to uphold. That foundation has to have time to cure, and it has to be tested, as in the backfill. But most of all, it has to stand the test of time. If it has no strength, it will not last. The weight will eventually overcome the structure, and everything built on it will come crumbling down. This is also true in men.

What am I talking about? There are so many aspects of life that we are responsible for that it can be overwhelming. But I believe there is a power in the structure that God set up for us, not only to survive but to thrive. I believe God knew what He was doing when He established man (and woman—it takes two), marriage, family, church, and community. In them, we find the components necessary to be successful and have a solid foundation on which to stand. In these components, there is unity to be solid, strength to bear weight, and there's balance to distribute the load. Although there are many benefits to standing on God's foundations, there are also many issues we have to deal with in the foundations that have been destroyed—like removing prayer in the schools and redefining the dynamics of the family. This is one of the reasons we need God's structure.

Have you ever heard the phrase "No man is an island?" The foundations I'm talking about take people—people with relationships. Relationships are established by associations. In each of the components of your foundation, you have agreements that establish those relationships, whether they are spoken or unspoken. Each relationship becomes a pillar that builds you up as a man. That's why we have to be so careful with what associations and relationships we have.

Here I will just list some of my thoughts about our

foundations. These are not all-inclusive or any kind of established theory. They're just things I think every man should think about as he develops his life's plan.

So let me throw this disclaimer out before I give it. For any woman reading these thoughts, don't take it personally or chauvinistically. These next few thoughts are for the *men!* I'm just giving some perspective. So maybe you should just skip to the next chapter while I talk to my brothers for a minute. But here it goes. It seems to me that men should tend to think long-term. I said *should!* Women think more in terms with the immediate, or the present.

When I say long term, I mean having the burden of caring for the success of the whole family and its health, wealth, and well-being for the long haul. Women are so much better at accomplishing these aspects of life on a day-to-day basis than we are. But in the absence of the true *man,* women have had to take on these roles as the leaders, breadwinners, mothers and fathers, and the direction givers. What's wrong with this picture, especially when there is a man involved in the relationship? Our failure to have a holistic view of our responsibility has left us unprepared to be the leaders God created us to be. Now, many women have been empowered by being better educated, better equipped, and better prepared to lead than many men are!

God told us to be fruitful. We look at terms like "be fruitful and multiply" (Gen 1:22 KJV) and take it to mean bringing babies in the world. It does mean that, but it also means to be producers. God has equipped us to produce anything we decide to produce. Why not produce what He has created you to produce? I've seen many cases where men refuse to do what God has called them to do; He'll usually find someone else to do it. In a lot of those cases, it'll be a woman who's equipped, prepared, and ready to go. Then we have the nerve to complain about how she leads and why she's there.

Sometimes our roles get so misguided that there's a breakdown in the whole structure. And we wonder why we see some woman dragging her man by twisting his ear in her hand, saying, "Come on, let's go!" OK, that's just a hypothetical visual. I hope we don't see that anytime soon. But you get the point! And I truly believe these situations are our own fault, as men.

Remember me asking the question, what's influencing your decision making? There are so many diabolical entities out there that want to break down family structure. When we are not aware of who we really are and what our responsibilities are, we allow those influences to do exactly that—break us down.

This is why I believe that most women can't quite understand the pressure of the full responsibility that's on a man. While she needs security and established foundations and is working every day to get it, she needs to have it right now! If not now, she needs to see the plan and know that the foundations are being built.

That in itself can be enough pressure to break a man. But what does she see—us pondering what to do next, no long-term plan, no execution, and no success. While she's looking for leadership and directions, she's getting nothing. Some women even go to the point of thinking that men just don't have it at all and refuse leadership from a man altogether. That's when we really have problems out here.

Sometimes we don't realize it, but that's the very thing that sends a woman running off to the arms of another man...or woman! Neither she nor anyone else can quite explain why! Oops, did I go there? I hope the women took my advice and did skip to the next chapter!

This is not the only issue that needs to be addressed in this discussion, but it's one that needs to be said. I'm not trying to further break down men, but if it helps someone, to God be the glory. I'm saying these things so we can recognize some of the situations our brothers have to deal with, if not ourselves. If you have another strong opinion on the breakdown of men, speak up or write about it, and let's find some viable solutions. This is the power of gathering as men and being brave enough to discuss, discover, and face our issues.

Oops, I think I just fell off of my soapbox and slipped into this area I'm so passionate about. Why? Because I've suffered from being broken down by some of the situations I'm talking about in this chapter in my own life. Thank God for having other men of God in my life that can help with perspective. OK, now give me a hand, and help me get back up on my soapbox so I can move on with this topic.

So, bothers, let me help some of you fellows out. As I mentioned, there are things I believe we as men should have our eyes on to build that solid foundation. I also feel it is our responsibility, with God's direction, to build it. So here are some foundations and the pillars that stand on them.

The number one relationship you must have is with God! I didn't say you need this relationship. I said you must have it. Without a relationship with God, you've already destroyed the foundation of everything you've ever hoped for. You may acquire a lot of things, like friends, riches, or material things, but none of it means anything without God. These are the pillars of establishing regular relationship with God:

Love: Oh, don't get all hokey on me; the Bible says God is love, and we are the object of His love. So if we are to be like Him, we have to learn how to love like He does, unconditionally!

Prayer: Even Jesus had a regular routine of daily prayer with His Father, God. Don't you communicate daily with the ones you love? Why not Him, as He loved us first? My mother really loves God. How do I know? She has held prayer meetings consistently for over fifty-five years! Ironically, her name is Omega, which means "the last." I don't look at her name as the last letter of the Greek alphabet, which it is; rather, I look at her as the one whose prayers will *last* for generations to come. We need to be able to put up what I call those eternal prayers! The reason I'm here right now and able to write this book is because of the prayers of this woman that I love so much!

Worship: The Bible also says that God is looking for ones to worship Him in spirit and in truth (John 4:23 KJV). Spending time in worship is the greatest thing that can bring you closer to God.

Trust: *Trust God!* "Trust in the LORD with all your

heart, and lean not on your own understanding; in all your ways acknowledge Him, And He shall direct your paths" (Prv 3:5–6 NKJV).

The next relationship is with yourself. You have to concentrate on and establish yourself as the best *you* that you can be. If you don't, you will shortchange yourself and everyone you have a relationship with, including God Himself. You will even limit what God can do for you. But when you are at your best, you feel good about yourself, and so does everyone else. You have to want to, plan to, and work to be the winner God made you to be.

Health: We have to be healthy enough to finish the race and to accomplish all God designed you to do. If for no other reason, get healthy to enjoy life and your family for as long as you can. As they say, this is a marathon, not a sprint.

Education: No matter what your education level is, do not stop the pursuit of learning. In my opinion, to stop learning is to stop living. We should learn something new every day. It keeps our minds vital, and it gives us something to pass along. Think of the things we've missed in our lives because of a lack of education, or things that others in our lives failed to pass on to us. Don't let another generation go by without the knowledge that you've gained in life! You are responsible for your own education. I repeat—you are the one person that is responsible for your own education. The system failed you, the teacher didn't like you, you went to a bad school, and…so what? There are many reasons for not getting it done. None of these are valid excuses for not educating yourself now. If you have the desire, you can find a way. There's enough free information on the Internet to have an education. Oh, you say you don't know how to use the Internet? Boom! You just identified your first self-study course!

Vocation: When women meet each other for the first time, they talk about the relationships in their lives: "Oh, I'm married or engaged" or "I have two children. I spend time with my mom" or "I'm involved with this or that." When men meet, they ask what each other does: "What do you do; where do you work or play or live." Men in general size each other up according to their vocations. Men usually feel good about themselves when they feel good about what they do and how well they provide for their families. To have a better vocation requires a better education. I don't just mean college—I mean a better education about yourself and about life and how to maximize your ability to provide yourself with that vocation. No matter what it is!

Outside of your relationship with God, your family is the most important relationship you have. I emphasize *your* family. As men, we have the responsibility of creating, sustaining, or being a part of a family until we create our own. As we get older, the more we understand the importance of family. God has a way of turning our hearts to family, whether you were born in a great family or not. Each member of the family has his or her role. There's a love that cannot be denied or changed.

Do you have what it takes to make a family? *Yes, you do!* Just because you may not have come from a solid family does not mean you cannot develop a solid family.

Even if you came from an environment where family was not established, you can and need to have family. If you have a family, get closer; you need each other. If there is dissension in the family, reconcile it, no matter what the cost. Because how family goes, men go. As men, I feel it is our responsibility to keep family, family. If you do not have a family, put yourself in the position to develop one. Love is the basis of family, and believe it or not, we as men need *love*! It can start with you loving one person at a time! Families are like living organisms—they grow! Believe it or not, our own future depends on family. We'll discuss that some later in the book.

- What does a family look like to God? This is a good topic for you to grab your Bibles and do a little research.

- What does a family look like to you? Write it down, and compare it to what you find in the Bible.

- What are the needs of the family? Are you prepared to position the family to meet its needs?
  - Food
  - Housing
  - Security
  - Education
  - Transportation
  - Insurance (all kinds)
  - Church home

When you look at all of these family needs, it's not surprising that many men bow out. That's why we need God and the church! When we were young, my dad used to tell my brothers and me all about the vast responsibility of manhood that will be on our shoulders. The better a man's ability to establish and manage these responsibilities, the better a foundation he builds.

The church is the next foundation we need. The church provides opportunity for the family to grow in God in a structured environment. All members of the family should be actively involved in the church. A lot of people look for what they can get out of being a member of the church, but in reality, you have more to give than you think. When you are active and serve in the church, the benefits are so much greater than the time and effort it takes to get involved. Jesus Himself made a promise to those that serve Him: "Whoever serves me must follow me; and where I am, my servant also will be. My Father will honor the one who serves me" (Jn 12:26 NIV).

Psalm 92:13 says, "Those who are planted in the house of the LORD Shall flourish in the courts of our God."

We must have a community relationship—families make communities, communities make cities, cities make nations. We are a part of the whole world. If we who are believers do not have a presence in the community, we leave the community and the world to those who are not influenced by the principles of God. We then will have to deal with our foundations being destroyed.

The challenge is this: in today's world, how do we develop relationships with God, self, family, church, and community all at the same time? We can't develop them all at the same time, especially when we have our own personal issues to deal with. That's why we must have a plan. It takes time and focus to be successful.

But with God, not only are all things possible, they are achievable. One thing we don't always realize is that when we go to church, everyone you see is in some stage of development in these areas. Some are further along than others, but none of us are what you would call "there."

To build any foundations, we must have confidence in God; and we must have confidence in ourselves.

About God, the Bible says, "And this is the confidence that we have in him, that, if we ask any thing according to his will, he heareth us" (1 Jn 5:14 KJV).

As for confidence in myself, this one scripture speaks to me in so many ways. Allow the various Bible translations of this one verse, 1 Corinthians 16:13, to speak to you.

KJV: "Watch ye, stand fast in the faith, quit you like men, be strong."

NKJV: "Watch, stand fast in the faith, be brave, be strong."

NLT: "Be on guard. Stand firm in the faith. Be courageous. Be strong."

NIV: "Be on your guard; stand firm in the faith; be courageous; be strong."

ESV: "Be watchful, stand firm in the faith, act like men, be strong."

MSG: "Keep your eyes open, hold tight to your convictions, give it all you've got, be resolute."

And finally, the Amplified version, which breaks it down and explains the verse: "Be alert and on your guard; stand firm in your faith (your conviction respecting man's relationship to God and divine things, keeping the trust and holy fervor born of faith and a part of it). Act like men and be courageous; grow in strength!"

I remember once in a heart-to-heart, man-to-man to man conversation with my father, he told me, "Never let anyone break your confidence. You have to be strong and believe in yourself. A man with his confidence broken makes it almost impossible to accomplish anything. Even if you doubt yourself, go forth strong like you have the army of God behind you."

When King David asked God if he should pursue his enemies after his biggest strategic failure, God told him to "pursue, overtake, and recover all." (1 Sa 30:8 KJV)

But notice David first went to God.

Periodically men must gather to strengthen one another, support one another, and learn from each other. Never tear down your brothers, and always rejoice in each other's victories. A famous poet named Rudyard Kipling wrote a very popular poem called "The Law of the Jungle" about the rules of living in a wolf pack.

Every man should look it up and read it. At the end of the second stanza is one of my favorite lines. It's an example for us as men, and it explains a whole lot about how much men need one another so much.

Now this is the Law of the Jungle
as old and as true as the sky;
And the Wolf that shall keep it may prosper,
but the Wolf that shall break it must die.

As the creeper that girdles the tree-trunk
the Law runneth forward and back
For the strength of the Pack is the Wolf,
and the strength of the Wolf is the Pack

Selah!

Kipling, Rudyard. *The Jungle Book*. New York: Sterling Publishing, 2007.

-Six-
THE GREATEST INVESTMENT

I asked God for wisdom, and He gave me wisdom. Conventional wisdom would have me to say, "I can't believe I'm even writing this book." Always the logical one, I knew I lacked wisdom. Many years ago someone told me that the Bible says, "He who lacks wisdom, let him ask" (Jas 1:5 KJV). So I began to pray for wisdom. Wisdom for what? I honestly did not know. But the One who created me knew. He knew exactly what I needed and why I needed it. He also knew it would be what many of you needed.

When I was a young boy, I noticed girls always seem to have secrets—secrets among themselves that always made it seem like they were so much smarter about themselves. Usually when a guy feels like this for the first time, they just kind of blow it off as, "Aw, I really don't care." The strange thing is that from that point on, it seems that boys are totally lost about who they are. They usually don't think about where they are in life or what's in store for them. Most of the time, they really don't care or give it much thought. It usually only comes up when that macho competitive urge is stirred up. The other time is when that special girl comes along and puts a twinkle in their eye.

Girls are taught all about their growth stages, from the time they hit puberty to the time they are old ladies with blue hair on their way to play bingo at the senior center. Girls learn from their mothers, their sisters, their friends, and any other woman willing to steer them in the right direction. They teach them from a physical sense, prepare them from a mental sense, and give them an awareness of the spiritual side of their life. This is why the church is about 60 percent or more filled with women. Because there is such a void of spiritual awareness in men, of the 40 percent that are there, half of them are there because their wives or girlfriends dragged them away from the football game, and they're watching the clock to see if they're going to make it home in time for the second game.

So by the time girls grow up and are ready to settle down and make a family, they have already been domesticated. From the time they've received their first baby doll, they are being taught and prepared for a domestic life. Once girls are acclimated to their first doll, they already understand that they are responsible for that doll. They know that they have to take care of this baby. They have to feed the baby, dress the baby, and even change the make-believe stinky diapers for this baby. When they have raised not only this baby doll but probably several others, the baby doll has grown up to become Ms. Barbie.

Now with this Ms. Barbie, the girls experience the full gamut of imaginary adult domestication. Ms. Barbie has met and dated Mr. Ken. They got engaged and planned a big wedding. They got married in a church and went on a honeymoon. They bought a house, a fancy car, a wardrobe, furniture, and a camper and went on exotic vacations. Now they can "play house." Now, I'm sure you know what happens when you "play house!" Well, if you don't know, here comes a Barbie baby shower. After all of this, the girls are ready to experience life for real.

Now here's this guy that this girl is about to settle down with. When he was a baby, they gave him a ball or car to push around or maybe even a brick—he didn't care. It didn't require much thought, let alone any responsibility. Then he learned to play baseball and sports. He learned to build camaraderie, and at some point in his upbringing, he learned to become competitive. Now, when he meets the apple of his eye, he has to learn the rules of engagement and must learn to hunt! She has now becomes his prey. All of a sudden, he has to become familiar with the dating *jungle*! Oh, it's a jungle all right, because he has no idea what he's doing.

By the time he figures out that he needs to *keep* this "womankind" that he's hunted down, he bends to the pressure of her domestication and pops the question. So now here he is, getting ready to get married. But first, he has to stop by the frat house so he can pick up his PlayStation 34 he's left there. Then he's gotta stop by his mom's to pick up his laundry he left there last week, because he ran out of underwear and can't turn the ones he has on inside-out anymore! Now here he is standing at the altar, at this big, expensive wedding that *she* planned, standing there like a *deer in headlights* going, "Duhhhh, what the heck am I doing here?"

Most men just aren't ready to start life at this point, but they do it anyway. We have not been domesticated and have no clue what we've just gotten ourselves into. All we want to know is, when does the honeymoon start? OK, now what? What's next—how do we get started? Where are the **blueprints**?

I was telling one of our newer pastors this story, and he was looking at me pretty funny, just smiling. As soon as I finished, he blurted out, "Man, I'm going to buy my son a Ken doll right now!" He said, "I'll tell his mother—don't worry about it, I got this! Man, we better get these boys ready quick."

GENERATIONAL INVESTMENT

As I began to seek out information for men, I found very little information and direction about the things women learn about life naturally. There was a lot of material about being a man, being responsible, and taking charge. I found a lot of information about the spiritual man, as far as a relationship with God, and a lot dealing with relationships as fathers, husbands, and sons. But at the time I could not find anything about what I call the "cycles of life for men." Nothing really talked about what's going on in someone's life at a certain age or the next stage of life.

I can look at some guys younger than myself and say, "Boy, I remember being at that stage—whew!" Man, I thought I knew something and didn't have a clue. Worse yet, I didn't even know that I didn't have a clue! Better yet, sometimes I look at older guys and wonder how old they are or what it's like being their age. What's his story? What will it be like when I get to that age? Will I even recognize when I'm getting there? I look at what I used to call "older men" and see their stature. I see some men very healthy and well, and some are very financially fit. Yet I see some with failing health or struggling financially or just trying to get by.

I thought about how little we think of ourselves when we're past the age of our vitality. By the time my legacy is carved in stone, and there's little I can do to change it, how will I feel about myself and what I have contributed to life? I started to take stock of my time and resources. After assessing myself, I was pretty disappointed in what I found. I definitely was not happy with where I was physically, and after having to start over a couple of times financially, I certainly wasn't where I should have been—especially not after working for forty years. I thought I was in good shape mentally, until I did this darn self-assessment, that is! And as far as spiritually, I felt like Paul in the Bible when he spoke of the fact that he could be boastful about being caught up into the third heaven, but he can't. How could he, looking at his current condition (2 Cor 12)? I know the Lord's grace is beyond sufficient for me. I feel blessed to even be able to partake in the revelations, or should I say illuminations, that God has shared with me.

I thought about some of the things I've done in my life. I know I've ministered and served many people. I may have made some minor impacts in a few churches I've attended. I've had an impact on my family. But I have to ask myself, have I made a dent in the assignment for which God has created me? I've had to look at the time I have left before my clock runs out. I needed to know, how can I make a difference? How can I become significant? How can I finish my assignment?

For all the athletic accolades we shoot for, the quest (or shall I say hunt) for that beautiful woman we want to brag on, or that business we started or the fast car or big house or whatever it is are in pursuit of—what is it that we're really going after? One thing I know for sure is that what we need is *significance*. I heard John Maxwell say, "Once you taste significance, success will never satisfy."

There are businessmen and actors, sports moguls and high achievers, factory workers, policemen, and even preachers who at some point in their lives must examine themselves. When the reality sets in that they have many more years behind them than they have in front of them, they usually will question their significance! Maybe we compare ourselves to others around us or those in our same age bracket, in our same economic status, or even our own family members. But at some point for sure, we will be looking in that mirror asking ourselves, what am I doing here, and what have I done?

Whenever this happens, we should be asking ourselves, where am I investing my time? I truly mean *investing* your time, not just spending your time. Just like with money, if you keep spending your time, time is going to run out. So if you're just spending your time frivolously with no accountability and no productivity, you will not be able to leave an inheritance for your children and your children's children. That's what the Bible tells us we should do. This is not only a financial inheritance but a spiritual one as well. What you deposit into your own legacy is based on where you've invested your time.

How we spend or invest our time is usually manifested

in our habits. Habits become our tendencies and create trends. Trends become prophetic and will predict what will happen to us and to our offspring. They are prophetic because they become the reality of your future and the future of the generations behind you. We have to think about the things that are passed down generationally. What we pass to the next generation does not stop once our sperm fertilizes the egg. We are continuously depositing into the lives of our offspring. How we utilize our time has an eternal influence on their lives. Earlier I mentioned the many years of my mother's prayers; do you think for a minute that her prayers have not had an influence in my life? They absolutely have and still do. So what are you doing that is affecting the lives of your children—or future children, if you do not have any already?

Speaking of investing time, a very close friend of mine wrote a book about serving time in preparation for life after incarceration. The title of the book is *Managing Time: The Inmate's Guide to Serving Time Productively.* The target audience is incarcerated men and women. The purpose is to encourage and equip them to serve their time productively so that those being released will be prepared to make the challenging transition from prison back to society.

In fact, this book is so impressive for managing your commitment to the disciplined focus and for investing your time in service to God that the foreword's author wrote, "The message is a timely one, and it isn't just words on a page for the incarcerated but practical insight into how each of us can honor God through managing time wisely."

INVESTED IN ME

As I was thinking about the time I've invested versus the time I've spent, I realize how much more I could have had in life. I asked myself the question about why I got into the time wasting and frivolous things I partook in. Then it came to me to look at the things that were invested in me. Sometimes in the church we talk a lot about generational curses—things spoken over your life or curses executed that are passed from generation to generation. But we must also look at things that are not curses but were just passed from our fathers and forefathers.

Consider this scripture: "I lavish unfailing love to a thousand generations. I forgive iniquity, rebellion, and sin. But I do not excuse the guilty. I lay the sins of the parents upon their children and grandchildren; the entire family is affected—even children in the third and fourth generations" (Ex 34:7 NLT).

This is not a curse but a proclamation from God to Moses about the depth of our sin. It can go to the third and fourth generation. And we wonder why we're prone to addictions, broken families, adultery, and even murder! If we could examine our forefathers, we may find all kinds of things that affect our lives. Without being aware of it, maybe you found yourself prone to gambling or some other addiction. Is that because you just liked it or it just happened to become a habit? Maybe somewhere in your DNA is this thing that was passed from previous generations. Once you've tasted or experienced gambling or whatever, you had the DNA in you to make it stick to you. I'm not saying this is in every case, but this has to be a strong consideration.

YOUR GREATEST INVESTMENT

I've covered most of the important things about investing your time. But I feel that other than God, my greatest investment is investing in myself. If I cannot invest in myself, I cannot be the best "me" that I can be. If I'm not the best me, then I cannot offer my best to help someone else, and I'm shortchanging myself and them.

I know we always preach to be selfless, but when we invest in ourselves in the right way, we have the right to be a little selfish. Why? Because in the end, it's the investment in yourself that determines your quality of life and your ability to pour into others. This is kind of an oxymoron. You have to be *selfish* and invest in yourself in order to be *selfless* and better able to invest in others. Investing in others is an essential part of your purpose.

So if you want to increase your ability to make a difference or give more, do more, give to charity, mentor someone, or give anything, you have to invest in yourself! When you do, you will have that much more to give. Think about it—you cannot give what you do not have. How do we give? You have to learn in order to teach; you must have money to give money; you must have love to give love; you must be at peace to offer peace; you must grow in order to grow someone else! To invest in others, you have to have a return on the investment in yourself.

In the Bible, John wrote a letter to a man named Gaius. In his greeting, he said, "Beloved, I pray that you may prosper in all things and be in health, just as your soul prospers" (3 Jn 1:2 NKJV).

It's obvious that Gaius was a very upstanding, successful man at the time. John's greeting is hoping that he is as healthy as he is prosperous in other areas in his life. If we endeavor to prosper in all areas of our lives, the quality of the end of our own lives will be so much better for our families and for ourselves. In this area, be selfish. Get better at whatever it is you are investing in yourself. Later I'll show you an example of the results of investing in yourself.

So the question is, how are you investing your time? What are you depositing into the future? Whether you are around to see it or not—it may be generations from now—but when the time comes, *you* are the one that determines what will be withdrawn by what you are depositing and investing.

We as men have to be able to focus on what the return is going to be on our time investment, or will we just be "spending time!"

The Bargain

I bargained with Life for a Penny,
and Life would pay no more,
However, I begged at evening,
when I counted my scanty store.

For Life is a just employer,
He will give you what you ask,
But once you have set the wages,
why, you must bear the task.

I worked for a menial's hire, only to learn, dismayed,
That any wage I had asked of Life,
Life would have willingly paid.

— Jesse Rittenhouse, as quoted in Napoleon Hill,
Think and Grow Rich, 1960, p. 40

-Seven-

SEASONS AND CYCLES OF LIFE FOR MEN

While evaluating our time or even ourselves overall, some men may not be able to make an accurate assessment. They may even lie to themselves, saying, "I'm doing pretty well," so they can feel pretty good about themselves. Maybe that's why some women believe in appeasing men's egos for the sake of getting what they want from us. For the most part, it works. Our egos can swell to the point of reality getting away from us. But as we assess ourselves, we have to have a proper perspective. Again, we have to ask ourselves where we have been in life and where we are going. A song of Moses asked God, "Teach us to number our days, that we may gain a heart of wisdom" (Ps 90:12 NIV).

It is always wise to number our days. What does it mean to number our days? It doesn't mean just go look at the calendar and see what day it is. But look at the calendar and ask yourself, what I have done in the last six weeks or last six months or the last year? Maybe look at the last five years. Then project forward six months, a year, and five years. Now look at it from your whole life perspective. There are many benefits in doing to this. You get a sense of your personal progress. It also gets you thinking about what's left for you to do.

I was meditating on my own situation when God began to steer my attention to the life cycles of men. As always, He started by piquing my curiosity. Then as I started researching, He gave me new perspectives. First He introduced me to the physical development of men. Later He started pointing me to the mental development. I asked, OK, Lord, what are you trying to show me? In time I realized that we were taught, according to scripture, that we are three-part beings made in the image of God. As I mentioned earlier, we are spirit, soul, and body. As men, we must realize as we age that all three parts of man grow, and not at the same rate or the same time. Our bodies grow in its own time, our mind grows in their own time, and our spirits grow in their own time. Each part develops at its own pace from one stage to the next.

We are always either at one particular stage in our lives or transitioning into or out of a stage. Once we reach a particular stage, we are usually empowered for that season in our lives. We can handle that. It's the time of transition that causes us to be nutcases and all discombobulated. We understand women's cycles of times when they are nuts. Because of their biological make-up, their times are very measured and predictable— monthly! But for men, their life cycles are from stage to stage and are not so predictable. It's not the same as for a woman, because there's no set time and no predictable pattern that we can pinpoint, except their age and the development of their life situation. So the progression of changes in a man's life is never the same for two different people. It is as individual as you are.

When our bodies begin to change, our minds may not be aware of the changes right away. A good example of that is when we go make some stupid bet that we can still dunk a basketball and try it. Then after we've paid off that stupid bet, we wonder what happened. We tell ourselves, "Well, it's just because I haven't done it in such a long time." Well, I hate to be the one to break the bad news to you, but *it's over—it's gone!* Or we get the shock of the first time our sons can beat us in basketball, for real. I mean, you were really trying to beat him and actually couldn't. Uh-oh! What happened? Our bodies out-aged our brains! When we do this, we're measuring ourselves against a younger, fresher body. It works the same way with our minds.

Your spirit can be crying out for attention or development while the body and soul are doing their own thing, not even aware of it. But thank God I'm a spirit, because as our spirit grows, we grow closer to God; but eventually, we need to be aware of the state of our spirit, soul, and body so we can operate accordingly and accomplish what we are designed to do. Being aware of these can help you make adjustments along the way and not trip into thinking we should do something because we think we can or want to feel like we can. I was a pretty good football player at one time, but I would be crazy to think that today I can suit up and step out on the field and go at it. I'd get carried off the field, dead or alive; either way, the truth will be told!

So the big question that we fail to ask or recognize is, where am I in life? What stage am I in right now? Maybe I'm in a transition. What's different about me now than one, two, or maybe five years ago? Guess what—you are not the same as you were one, two, or five years ago. Nor are you the same as you will be one, two, or five years from now. The problem is that we will go through many changes and not be able to fully identify when or where we've changed or where we've been or where we are going next. We usually find out after we get there and then have to figure out how to operate in that stage. "Man, I've been working out for two months and still can't dunk that ball anymore. Ouch!"

I don't want anyone to think that this information is the result of some major scientific study or research. This work is nowhere near where I consider it all-inclusive or even an authoritative guide. But I hope it inspires you to think of your life's situations that may not even be documented here. Let's take those situations and articulate them in a way where other men can take advantage of them. I just feel obligated to pass on some of my experiences to help incite some thought in this area, where there is so little information. This is all the result of God challenging me with questions about my own life. He's giving me experiences with others, and I'm challenging myself to recognizing a need, be creative, and find a solution, just like I've admonished you to do in chapter one.

STAGES OF LIFE FOR MEN

To explain what I call the cycles of life, I've outlined interesting points about the ones I could identify with. To give some clarity to some of the terms I'll use, here's a few words that I use to describe the process. These may seem simplistic, but just to set a level, having the correct definition may become important when we see how to use this information as we move forward.

Progression: the process of developing over a _—on-going_ period of time; a continuous and connected series of actions, events, and the like (like a view of the whole set of stages)

Stage: a particular point or period in the growth or development of something

Transition: movement, passage, or change from one position, state, subject, or concept to another; the process of change

Our overall progression consists of transitioning from stage to stage. We are at a stage for a particular season, and then things start to change. When things start to change, we go into the transition period until we land on the next stage. These transitions are usually our toughest seasons. This is because we have not adjusted to the changes taking place. Most of the time, we don't even realize that the process of changing from one stage to the next has even started. Sometimes it takes a while to recognize that our status quo is not working for us anymore, and we wonder what's wrong. Sometimes we misdiagnose the real issues when we identify the problem as everyone but ourselves. But the real issue is you. Is it your body changing or your mind-set in the "soulish" realm? Is your spirit perceiving things differently now? I say yes, yes, and most likely yes!

These are the stages of life that we'll try to deal with at some level. The list is not all-inclusive but includes the major ones. The point here is to get you to think about your life—also your father's or sons' lives—in terms of recognizing life's changes from stage to stage and identifying events and decisions that have shaped our lives to the point where we are today.

The ages I associate with the stages are approximate ages. They are not carved in stone. These are just my observations, and the actual ages of these stages vary from one man to the next, depending on many factors around us.

THE STAGES
Prebirth:
This is the time before you are born. Duhhh, now that didn't take rocket science to figure out, did it?

What do we know about life before we are born? One thing for sure is we are one in a million—actually, more like one in 250 million. When a man's sperm is released, there are upward of 250 million sperm released, each racing to get to the promised land before his slimy little brethren. But in every case, of every person ever born, they were the winner in that race. What does that tell you? You didn't win that race because you were the fastest swimmer or because you would be the cutest baby! *Not!* But you were chosen by God to be the one born at that time. And that in itself makes you a winner. Whether you feel that are or not, God said, you are a winner! "But as many as received Him, to them He gave the right to become children of God, to those who believe in His name: who were born, not of blood, nor of the will of the flesh, nor of the will of man, but of God" (Jn 1:12–13 NKJV).

There is a lot of controversy in the world about when life really starts. Any information we have about the start of life is derived from scientific discoveries of the physical evidence from the body. But of course I have an opinion on that. I believe the physical life starts when that sperm race ends and the eggs are fertilized. That's when life begins to grow. At what other point in time can we divide the physical aspect of development and the start of life? For surely a child in the womb of a woman is a life of its own.

The only real reference to preconception is the Bible itself. Aside from the physical start of life, according to the Bible, God conceived us in His mind way before we were born. As a matter of fact, the biblical evidence lets us know that He conceived us before He even created the world. It doesn't say we were created at that time, but it does show evidence that He knew us, called us, and ordained us (Jer 1:5, Is 49:1–5, Rom 8:29).

This is important to understand because we have an affinity to our Creator—an indescribable connection that most of us have never even considered. I wonder if we have ever thought about this relationship like this: "Before I knew who I was myself, my Creator knew me, knew what I would become, knew the decisions I would make, and more importantly, knew the person He created me to be! He knows me. That's why I can go to Him in prayer and be open and comfortable. He knows me better than I even know myself."

Selah!

Childhood (infant to nine):
This is the state or period of being a child; the early stage in the existence of something. This where we come into life, totally dependent on the foundations of our parents. The foundations, meaning relationships with God, family, church, and community, determine

our quality of life in the early years and make such a huge difference in the overall developmental process.

The most important experience children have when they come into the world is a loving, nurturing relationship with their fathers and mothers. It's the same with us adults, by the way (see relationship with God in an earlier chapter). Just like infants, we need to have the love of our fathers, the nurturing that tells us we're safe, and the assurance that we'll eat and be warm in the comforts of our savior's arms.

I always say that the education systems fail in two major areas. One is teaching the importance of God in our lives. They took prayer out of the schools, and we wonder why there's so much destruction in our schools and society. Today that responsibility is left to parenting, and parenting without God leads to a broken world. The other failure is not teaching our children how to learn. By that I mean teaching them to learn for themselves, especially when there is no teacher. We teach children to memorize a lesson for the sake of passing a test, not to learn the content of the lessons and build on what they learn. The system needs to start really early in teaching children to take responsibility for their own education by learning how to learn on their own!

I know that sounds funny, but the early stages of life are the greatest opportunity to teach children how to learn. I believe that if you teach them to pursue understanding and learning, teaching them would be a whole lot easier for the rest of their lives. Let's teach them how to figure things out at an early age and at a developmentally appropriate rate.

This is when they should start to learn about who they are and whose they are—they are children of God. If they get an understanding that they are children of God, then we should never have to worry about them understanding or choosing what is right or wrong.

It normally takes seven years for children to form their personalities and characters. This is when it is most important to instill in them the character and standards by which they will live.

7 yrs to form a child's character

I believe in discipline, but your child is not in the military and is not a whipping post. I believe spanking is OK, but not to the point where it can be considered abusive. Let your children be children. Let them know the hearts of their fathers. That's why I think that all men should be in the delivery room at the birth of their children. I believe this makes a big difference in the love and care they feel for that child. I believe there would be fewer abandoned and fatherless children. It's hard to tell men that they would love their children more if they were present at the birth. But no matter how tough or how macho you are, there's just a little something extra about that birth that grabs your heart and makes it twitch when you think about the fact that this is what you made!

Preteen (ten to twelve):
This is the period between childhood and adolescence. This when the awkward stage of puberty kicks in. Puberty is the period of life when a person's sexual organs mature and he or she becomes able to have children; in common law, presumed to be fourteen years in the male and twelve years in the female. The changes in the body and the mind are drastic. This is

the time when the most nurturing needs to take place. It's also the oddest time, because this is when the least amount of nurturing is desired. For the first time, they don't want to be attached to Mom or Dad. How do you make that work? By just being sensitive to the changes and making sure perspectives are guided and godly standards are being set.

The earlier you set the standards, the easier they will be to enforce later when they're needed. Things like curfews and phone and social media habits. Monitoring the types of gaming and online activities is a must. This was not an issue many years ago, but today it is commonplace for the media world to overtake our youth. This is when children have to be opened up to the world by someone with moral standards to establish moral standards in their own lives. If our children are left to be exposed by the world, they'll think we have no clue to their reality. We have to get them to understand that these things are the way of the world and lead to their destruction. It's easier to keep them from falling than letting them fall into it and trying to pull them out of it.

How do we do this? Start with the habit of praying together about the issues that face our youth. Pray with our young men to lead them to not be afraid of taking a role in living righteously. Have them openly participate in praying what's on their hearts. Teach them not to be afraid to address the tough issues, and explain the diabolical plans for the things they are being exposed to. We cannot help the world raise godless children!
This is the beginning of them starting to establish their own foundations of having a relationship with God. This will go a long ways in the coming teen years,

where this foundation will be very important in their lives.

So I hear some of you asking, What do I do now that my child is in the preteen years, and I don't didn't do those things early on? Find a way to start doing them now. It's not too late, and the value you add will be lifelong. Admit you didn't know, and now you do, and move on.

Adolescence (thirteen to eighteen):
This is the transitional period between puberty and adulthood in human development, extending mainly over the teen years and terminating legally when the age of majority is reached. The a*ge of majority* refers to the legal age of adulthood. The age of majority varies in different countries and even in different jurisdictions within a country. It also differs with the type of activity concerned, such as marrying, purchasing alcohol, military service, or driving an automobile. Twenty-one years is a common division between minors and adults.

The teen years are the ages of the most influence in the development of men. Believe it or not, what happens in these years can determine the level of difficulty of life as a man. Two major transitions have to take place in this stage: the period of time from childhood to teenager, and from teenager to man.

In childhood, you are standing on the foundations of your parents or caretakers, but leaving the teenage stage is where you're being torn away from the parental foundations. When moving from parental foundations, you land somewhere in the unknown, on shaky ground, where life is uncertain and not guaranteed. These are

the ages where your body begins to outgrow your brains (soul). Eventually, in the later part of the teen years, your brain will grow at a faster rate to catch up to your body.

If boys in this age group are not spiritually grounded, the influences of the world will overtake them and swallow them into the diabolical systems of the world. We wonder why we lose so many young men to gangs, drugs, pornography, prison, and homosexuality. Sometimes it leads to just being wanderers with no direction. This is where it takes real men to be a greater influence to these young men more than anything there is in the world. This is not an easy task.

Then there are those that seem to have it all together, doing the right thing as far as school and progressing toward building themselves up as model citizens, sports figures, or famous people. But be careful; you also have to watch who or what is influencing these young men also. These type of young men become the targets also. They can easily be drawn into dark side of life from a self-centered, "what's in it for me" perspective, all in the pursuit of success. There is so much acceptance and promotion of witchcraft and sorcery in our society today. Those that operate in this darkness, use media and whatever means they can to indoctrinate our youth into thinking this darkness is a good thing or harmless. Either case is just as damaging as the other.

There has to be an established and trusted relationship to keep the attention of these young men. Their perspective must be tested and challenged—challenged in a good way. There must be checks, balances, and rewards. And most of all, they must be rooted and grounded in God's word. When these things are not in the life of the teenage male, he's fighting an uphill battle.

The number one characteristic that a young man needs is *love!* In this, he should be steered in the right direction yet while being allowed to somewhat find his own way. If he has no relationship with a real man, it will be hard for anyone to steer him. Once he experiments with some things and has what he may call success (what's fun or popular), it's hard to tell him he's wrong and headed for destruction.

This age group goes through the most physiological and rapid changes of any group. Most boys in later phases of this group find their sexual awakening. This is where they can learn to respect their sexuality, or they can learn to abuse it. This awakening is a transition from the initial stages of puberty, signifying that the person is no longer a child but a real *man*—wahoo! (Insert flexing some new muscles right here.) Sometimes this change comes with a little attitude and rebellion, because he is trying to flex his "I'm growing and I can get away with it" muscle. It takes a little while to settle into this phase.

Again, what foundational habits are being formed or have been formed at this stage?

I remember a case where there was a young man about seventeen years old, about to turn eighteen. He was sexually abusing and controlling his girlfriend, openly and publically. After being informed about this young man, I had a talk with him. Well, a stern, come-to-daddy, what-the-hell-are-you-doing kind of talk.

He had done what so many others in his position have done. There was no man in his life to teach him about the transition into real manhood. He found some girl to take advantage of who also had no man in her life to teach her from a father's heart. She became someone looking for the attention of a man. This is what happens when there are no men our girls' lives. I've had occasions to speak with the mothers and daughters when the girls were going off to college. I tell them, "If you encounter a boy who's interested in you, talk about the men in your life. Even if there are none, use the men in the church or a relative or any man you know really well." Young guys will treat her a whole lot differently if they think she has men in her life that she respects. If a guy thinks she's covered by a man, he knows he cannot abuse and control her without having to be confronted. Otherwise she is fair game, and he feels like he can do whatever he wants with her. This is why we have to cover every young girl we know that does not have a real father in her life. This has to be an honest, godly relationship that has governance or oversight.

This is what happened with this young man I had to approach. I had to teach him in a few moments about the disrespect he showed this girlfriend, her mother, his mother, the church, and most of all himself. This later stage of adolescence is the approximate time when your body outgrows your brain. You have the body of a growing man but the brains of a kid who found the keys to the candy store.

Many people tried speaking to him, punishing him, chastising him, or controlling him to no avail. I had to break what was going on down for him. At this age there was an overload of testosterone building in his system. Although he was a football player, he did not know what was driving him to crave sex and desire power and control. Nor did he know how to deal with it. This was where intelligent wisdom had to come into play. Some people would say, "Go home, and take care of it yourself." I say that's the wrong answer. That can be as damaging as his current situation. I explained to him how to avert his desires and energy in other ways.

What should our teenage boys be doing at this stage in their lives? This is where the importance of establishing the good habits of building the foundations I spoke of earlier comes into play. Teen boys need to have balance in their lives. Without good examples, their minds become controlled by their bodies, instead of the other way around. I told this particular boy he needed good sleep habits and good hard exercise routines where he could really push himself. He needed to concentrate on his studies and other mind-challenging or developing efforts. He needed to find an enjoyable outlet.

Football season was over, so he needed to get into other activities, like learning new skills that could be rewarding for his future. He needed to be creative and find a way to use those new skills to make some money, legitimately. It was also important that he find a mentor that could teach him about what real respect is and how to respect and treat a real girlfriend. I told him that when he found someone that was in his girlfriend's situation, he should teach her how a real man is supposed to treat her instead of abusing her.

This is an age group where the mind can absorb information at a very rapid pace. If the mind is left to be guided by the world, it will be fed by the world. But what we need is prayer, prayer, and more prayer. Not for the sake of saying, "Oh, we're going to pray about it," but praying for direct and creative answers and direction.

There was much more to be taught in this case, but this is not the only case where teenagers are misguided by media and influences of the world. It's so important to connect with this age group, because this is the first turning point that can shape the rest of their lives. So many lives are ruined because of boys being left to their own devices.

There are so many boys being raised by mothers without fathers in their lives, or fathers without the know-how to raise boys—nothing against the mothers out there. They've done the best they can to walk boys to the doorstep of manhood. But I believe they cannot cross them over into manhood, no matter how hard they try. I believe it takes a real man to take a boy over the threshold of manhood. Without it, there will be something missing in his life.

Young Adult (nineteen to twenty-seven):
Continuing from the teen years...Why do we need that man to bring us over into manhood? We need affirmation of being a real man. We need that pat on the back that says "go for it." When we enter manhood without the strength of that affirmation, we spend the rest of our lives either looking for approval or trying to prove our manhood to ourselves and everybody else.

We spend our college-age years trying to forge our identities. We're looking for acceptance as men. But there's still a whole lot of kid in us. As I describe this, I realize that most people in this age range really have no idea what they're looking for. They're just really trying to find out what life is all about. Most of what they find at these ages is pretty much quite a surprise. Their brains are processing things differently now. They never really feel like they're there. This can be the longest period of transition that we face in life.

In the United States, our young people go through a very tough period where they're asked to make major decisions for their lives at seventeen and eighteen years old. They are asked to make choices about college, careers, or military service. To be honest, I do not believe their brains are developed well enough to make these decisions.

The psychological and medical communities have determined that the full personality expression, decision making, and planning complex cognitive behaviors are developed in later stages in the frontal lobe of the brain. This development doesn't begin to mature until the twenty to twenty-five year age range. MRI studies of the developing brain show it isn't until the midtwenties or later when the physical development of the prefrontal cortex is complete.

This puts an inordinate amount of pressure on the child, parent, community, and the church. Again, this is the age where the help of the fathers and father figures is most needed. It's like after adolescence, life is starting over for them.

When we were visiting the Western Wall in Israel, also known as the Wailing Wall, there was a military graduation taking place there. We found out that the young men and women in the graduation would be entering college soon. Why? Because there, all the young men and women have to do two years of military duty before going into their undergraduate studies. This means that they are a little more mature, understand discipline, and have some experience in operational tasks and accomplishments. They are better equipped to make the life-altering decisions required by young people at this time.

I've seen various statistics indicating that from 50 to 80 percent of US college students change their majors at least once. This also indicates that there are plenty of students changing majors multiple times.

This is why at this stage, we have to find a way to teach our children that we have to trust the words in the Bible that tell us not to depend on our own understanding but to trust in God, and He will direct us: "Trust in the LORD with all your heart; do not depend on your own understanding. Seek his will in all you do, and he will show you which path to take" (Prv 3:5–6 NLT).

Separation Anxiety
Young men in this age group coming out of high school need to be integrated into a structured system—a system that offers some level of discipline and development, such as a college or university, a military organization, or even trade school. It is very important for these young men to continue to develop and discipline their minds and their bodies. They feel the need to develop the responsibility for their own lives. Even in a structured environment, they are responsible for their own successes or failures. Many young men

that are not successful—for whatever reason—usually blame someone else or some other situation for their lack of progress. That's why young men need to be led into the proper structured situation. Hence the Israeli military system.

When there is no definitive transition into a development system, there comes an onset of what I call separation anxiety. At this point, a young man's mind is driven to the very thing he needs the most: development. The first thing he wants to do in this case is leave home, looking to build his own foundation to stand on. In most cases, he's so unprepared to make good decisions and solid choices. He just wants to get away enough to be on his own so he can do what he wants to do. So what is that? Many young men find themselves running into something that's a mystery, but they run to it with rose-colored glasses on, partially because they are so uncomfortable where they are. They're standing on Momma's foundation or Daddy's foundation, and they began to feel that foundation being really shaky. Well, I hate to tell you, but it's not the foundation that's so shaky, it's the mind that's really shaky at this point.

This usually leads to thinking, "If I can get out of here, I can do this, or I'm gonna do that." They want responsibility for themselves, but what they are looking for is to lose the accountability. There is a big difference in having responsibility and accountability. In a structured system, they are accountable to authority. Outside of a structured system, they're accountable to no one. Young men, hear me: you will always, always be accountable to someone! Responsibility does not come without accountability, no matter where you go in life. If there is no accountability, at some point you will find yourself in serious trouble. You must be accountable to someone!

This separation anxiety will cause young men to take jobs where they're underpaid because of a lack of experience and knowledge. Or it may lead to jobs where they're misleadingly overpaid, again because of a lack of knowledge. I know that sounds the same, but these jobs usually require hard labor or hard work or effort that will lock them in for many years to come.

My dad used to tell us, "Boy, you stay a boy as long as you can, because once you become a man, you're a man for the rest of your life." Believe me, there is no turning back! He said this for us to really think about what we're doing or what decisions we're making for our lives. Are you ready to take on the responsibility that goes along with being a man? Do you understand the financial side of starting your own domain? When you go out on your own, you are starting your own domain. Your domain goes from just you to you and girlfriend or wife and children and bills and career and house and car—and so on and so on. Do you have the discipline to only buy what you can afford? Finances are a touchy subject with a lot of people. But you have to learn one of the principles that I've heard many successful people say about finances.

You first need to make tithing a non-negotiable policy in your life. Secondly, as diligently as you tithe, tithe to yourself. So the first 10 percent of your earnings goes to God, The second 10 percent of your earnings goes to yourself for savings, and you live off the other 80 percent. I know that sounds hard, but if you start it as a practice from the beginning, it won't be an issue from then on, especially if your domain is growing. You'll thank God in the long run. You see, when you tithe, God adds blessings to the point where your remaining 80 percent will accomplish so much more than you can with the 100 percent. Don't believe me? Try it!

If you're reading this and find yourself in this situation where you're undisciplined or you have separation anxiety, you must regroup. You need to sit down with a trusted person that has your best interests at heart to discuss and develop a plan for your life. This needs to be someone experienced and knowledgeable about helping you build proper foundations for your life. Again, I'll use this passage: "Unless the LORD builds the house, they labor in vain who build it; unless the LORD guards the city, the watchman stays awake in vain" (Ps 127:1 KJV).

Adulthood (twenty-eight to thirty-nine):
I wanted to spend some time in this age group, because this is the age range that can make or break a man for the next ten to fifteen years. The transition into this stage finds young men unaware they are changing. Many fail to understand that this next stage even exists. All they know is, "I'm turning thirty," without any idea what that means. Here is where we start evaluating whether we have a foundation. Most men at this age either feel they have it all together or have a "NAC" for where they are (NAC means "not a clue"). Those that feel like they have it all together feel like they can do anything. Those with a "NAC" feel like they can do anything. What's the difference, you ask? The resources available to do it.

They say that during midlife crisis is the time when

most men cheat. I say the twenty-eight to thirty-six age group is the age when the most infidelity occurs. I mentioned this to someone, and they asked, "Why, is it because of their ego or something?" I said, "No, it's kind of like when a woman without children has her 'biological clock' ticking." The only reason we know about the proverbial biological clock is because women identify this in each other and trumpet it or announce it when they confide in each other. Why can't we as men recognize our own biological clock? See, it's not just ego or that you're just perverted or always "horny" and have to be on the hunt. It's physiological and psychological! When we do not have the foundations built in our lives so that we feel at peace in where we are, we are looking for our own self-gratification and comfort.

Here we find ourselves in transition. This is where that discombobulation comes in. We're going from young adult to full adulthood. The transition can be shocking. It doesn't necessarily make sense, but it's reality.

It's not having self-satisfaction in our level of significance. If we lack in our perception of a solid foundation and don't have the proper balance in our development, we start seeking instant gratification...in all the wrong places. We want gratification for our view of significance, but it looks so far away from us. We start looking for the quick fix, like for a drug. Our minds get so distorted that we don't even know what it is we're looking for. Sometimes this chase leads to another woman, porn, drinking, isolation from our wives or family, or sometimes just being the "big man on campus" with your buddies. Whatever it is, it's a distraction from your proper life development—an interruption in you finding yourself in the name of finding yourself. Recognize that if this is where you are in age or mind-set, find your escape! Get out of it. Run! There's a scripture that says, "No temptation has overtaken you that is not common to man. God is faithful, and he will not let you be tempted beyond your ability, but with the temptation he will also provide the way of escape, that you may be able to endure it" (1 Cor 10:12).

You do not have to go into this mode in your life, and if you have, believe it or not, God has an escape route for you. I didn't say it would be easy or painless, but there is an escape. That's why I encourage you to fellowship with real men, because although it doesn't seem like it, it's a whole lot easier to stay out of this situation than it is to fall into it and need an escape. How do we escape? The first thing is you have to want it. Sometime we get so stuck in the very thing that's driving us in a hole that we don't recognize how much it's destroying us. Even when we know it's wrong, we tell ourselves, "I'm gonna get myself together" or "I'm not hooked; I can stop whenever I want to or need to." What does that sound like? Does that sound like a drug addict? Are you addicted to the thing that is killing you spiritually?

The Cheater
I'm not saying here that every man in this age group is a cheater, but for every man that has cheated on his spouse and (so-called) gotten away with it, let me give you a different perspective. In the Old Testament of the Bible, God uses the children of Israel as example of an adulterous bride by illustrating how they seemed to always turn to other gods. In the New Testament, the church today is the example of the bride of Christ. Now,

God also used the marriage as a microcosm of the relationship between Christ and the church (Eph 5). So how you treat your wife should be how you want God to treat you!

Here's the other perspective. When you got married, you and your wife became one. So what you do to her, you do to yourself. Think about it. As a married person, you have the unique ability to go to God for both of you, and so does she. She can intercede not just *for* you but *as* you. You are one. This is why you have to be the priest of your house, because you have to go before God for your household. Now, what are you taking to God? Remember Adam? In his sin, he ran from God. How did that work out for him?

There has to be someone in your life that you can discuss this issue with, either someone that has overcome these issues, or has an understanding of it. This person can become what we call an accountability partner. This is someone you can be accountable to when those hard days come, those days when the temptation and stress are hardest to deal with it. The last thing I want to see is your wife or family or potential family suffer from not knowing why you're going through this. Yes, it does affect your family. Remember, if you're not the best you can be, then there's no way those in your domain can be the best that they can be! Again, as men, we either cripple or uphold the health, wealth, and well-being of everyone around us in the domain that God has placed us over. You say you don't have a domain? You may not be able to identify it right now as father, mother, children, grandma, and grandpa; but are you going to limit what God has for you in the way of a family?

Measure your effect on your family. Some of the questions are, could this be why I don't have a family? Is this why my wife is always so angry or sensitive? Is this why my kids are so messed up? Guess what. Our families and our domain are a reflection of ourselves. Whatever you say your perception or assessment of your family is, take that same perspective and say the same thing about yourself. If you don't like what you say about them, then you don't like that same thing about yourself. Most likely they are the way they are because you are the way you are. Let's face it. To institute change, you have to start with you! So how do you do that? Number one, be honest with yourself. Two, *stop* whatever it is you've fallen into. Stop! How do I stop, you ask? Start by repentance. That's asking God for forgiveness—praying and asking God to send you some help. I know it sounds corny or cliché, but it works! He will put someone in your life that understands the dynamics of the situation you are in.

The main issue here is that you are in a spiritual eclipse and don't even realize it. When we are in this state, we are so unaware of our spirituality that we either forget God in our lives, or we ignore Him, thinking we can get away with it. This is when you need God the most. Remember reading about Adam hiding from God? We need to run to God. Why? Because in a spiritual eclipse, darkness is overshadowing the light (of God) in our lives. And most of all, we have to want change. Think about it. If you are not in this situation, maybe you once were and can help somebody who is. A former pastor used to tell us that free men, free men. Meaning it takes a free man, a man who has been liberated or freed from bondage, to be able to free someone who is still in captivity.

Sexball
OK, let me take a diversion from my topic for a minute to relate something that popped in my head one night. I have no idea why I woke up with this thought, but here goes.

Men and women have two different perspectives of sex. Women connect with the relational context of sex, where men relate to the recreation side of sex. Men can and usually must deal with the relational side. But they deal with the relational side better outside of the bedroom, especially leading up to the bedroom. So I have an analogy of a fictitious game called sexball. This analogy is the story of the sex life of a married man. This is a different way to explain the plight or struggles of men dealing with their sex lives in marriage.

I am using football as model for the sexball game—just because I like football! I wanted to use tennis or golf, because those are individual sports. Well, tennis wouldn't work because tennis is not a contact sport; sexball is. In golf, you don't have to play against anybody. You play against your personal best or against a group of people trying make the cut or get the best match score. You say football is not an individual sport? Well, shut up. This is my analogy! Now, football *is* an individual contact sport called sexball!

Here we go! Sexball has two individual teams with one player on each side. The players are called husband (male) and wife (female). The husband's team is named the Kings, and the wife's team is called the Queens. Both teams are in a league called the Marriage Sexball League (MSL). Now, the Queens' owner treats the team like the Yankees; they get everything. And the

Kings' owner treats them like the Washington Generals! Yeah, you know the ones. The same guys who've lost over fourteen hundred games to the Harlem Globetrotters. OK, just kidding, scratch the Yankees and Generals stuff. But that's how we feel sometimes.

In the game of sexball, there are two types of games you play. One is called "have sex," and the other is called "make love." So when the time comes to play, the teams negotiate to determine which type of game to play, when to play it, and the how to play the game. Well, this is where men begin to lose the game. Not really, because even when we lose, we win. But the Queens have all the advantages. Why? Because we want to play more than they do. So that puts us at a disadvantage. Why? Because God made it that way. So don't ask; league rules! No, you're not just a pervert or addict or some kind of freak; well, most of us aren't, anyway. But that's just how God made it, and that's just how it is. So deal with it!

Anyway...the Queens have the upper hand; we have to play the game by their rules. Yes, they conspire with the league and draft the game rules! Here's how the MSL negotiation goes between the Queens and the Kings. The MSL and the Queens set the following rules:

- They determine when we play. "OK, honey, I'll be right there!"
- They not only determine when we play but whether we'll play at all! "OK, I'll wait!"
- They determine whether we'll have a "rain" delay. "OK, maybe next week!"
- They want to make love; we want to have sex. "OK, make love it is!"

- They determine the requirements to get in the game. "OK, let me go get some flowers and some chocolate!"

Now, the MSL has determined that for the Kings to remain in the league, there are certain rules we have to adhere to:

1. You cannot play with any other team.

2. As a matter of fact, you cannot even look at another team, and you definitely can't watch another game on TV.

3. You cannot engage in any trade talks.

4. You can't even participate in any draft or scouting of any new players.

If you want to play, you have to meet all the conditions of the league:

1. First, no practice.

2. If you commit a foul, you forfeit the game and are suspended indefinitely—or until the Queens say so.

3. Since you're on suspension, you may be tempted to scout another team at the club mixer. But you better not.

4. You might be tempted to sneak in a practice game with another team or even a solo practice. But no, you better hold out. See rule number one.

Since you have no other options, you have to approach the Queens for reinstatement into the league. Eventually you've determined that in order to win, you must learn how to play within the rules, and if you ever want to play again, you will learn how to make love and appreciate that style of game. In the long run, maybe she'll even learn how to have sex. Now it's game on! So if we stick to the rules, maybe after a while, when it's time to retire and we can't play the game anymore, we both will have already gained a greater appreciation for the league, and we both win!

Although this is just a fun analogy, we as men have to realize that marriage is not a game but serious business. God's business. This is something we have to get right, because the intent is to be married for the rest of your lives. We have to respect marriage and enjoy it. Life will be so much better for you and everyone involved in your life.

Midlife (forty to fifty-five years):
Turning forty can be scary. I've always heard that life doesn't start until you're forty. Then you see all the "over the hill" banners and streamers they put up to so-called celebrate your arrival. But what do they know that I don't know? All I know is that I feel like I'm busy as ever and don't seem like I'm getting any traction for anything I really want to do. It's always either work or the wife and kids or over involvement—or sometimes it feels like I'm just spinning in circles. Hey, I know what, I'll use the old midlife crisis as an excuse to do something outlandish. Hey, they expect it at this age anyway, right? Wrong!

In actuality, what they call a midlife crisis only affects a very small amount of men. This is really not a crisis but a change in mind-set brought on by different pressures in life. But before we go there, lets back up—what happened? How did I get here? What happened to my twenties and thirties? I feel like I should still be in my early thirties, but I don't feel like it. It seems like the harder I work, the harder it is to maintain things I care about, like my job, my physical health, keeping my wife or girlfriend happy—oh, gee, that's a never-ending fight. Where did she come from anyway? That's not the woman I married or originally got involved with (in the case of a girlfriend if you're unmarried).

Anyone in this position is definitely steeped in a transition from one stage to the next, which is a very uncomfortable position. As a matter of fact, most of this stage can be very uncomfortable for some men. It's at this point where we find the second group of men most involved in infidelity. I'm not saying all men, nor am I saying most men. But there is a subset of men that fall in this category. It's easy to get caught up in a bad relationship at this point, because it's an easy, mindless escape from reality and the responsibility that you're looking for detachment from. You tell yourself, I just need a break. This is one of the reasons why there are so many strip clubs sucking in so many hard-earned dollars. If you are a patron of any of these establishments, *stop!* You are destroying yourself in the process.

This midlife behavior is a by-product of *narcissistic* tendencies, or the thinking that reflects an attitude of "it's about what I want and my needs" along with poor impulse control. This type of thinking will lead to all kinds of distractions. These distractions are just that—distractions. They will keep your mind so messed up you will not be able to grow, especially if you call yourself a Christian. If that is you, stop right now, and pray a prayer of repentance, asking God for forgiveness and help in this area. That's why we have to be accountable to one another. God has already provided a way out. You just have to find it.

"No temptation has overtaken you except what is common to mankind. And God is faithful; he will not let you be tempted beyond what you can bear. But when you are tempted he will also provide a way out so that you can endure it" (1 Cor 10:13).

Again, they say life doesn't start until you're forty. I believe it's because by now, you should have some sense of direction your life is going and be in hot pursuit of it. If that's true, wonderful. Just be sure it's the pursuit that God is directing you toward. At this point, most men should be at a place where they've established some foundation under them as far as career, housing, family, and lifestyle. You now have some traction in life where you can make some things happen. You have some experience in life, and now you begin to see things a little differently.

You should actually start seeing growth from all the hard work you've put in so far. You should be able to support some of the decisions you've had to make. You should see some results from some of the things you're investing in. Not just financially but in people, in your career, and in yourself. Now, if those investments were good investments, you should start seeing a harvest. Guess what, if those were bad investments, you should still start seeing a harvest. Look at where you are, and you will see the results of where you have invested. If you've only invested in recreation or things that don't grow you, you'll see the results. If you don't see progress at this point, you may be missing a sense of direction and of what can be profitable for your life.

Some men feel like they've found their paths to pursue,

and at this point, they are working very hard to get somewhere. Then some men have not found that path and are still working hard. I think work ethic increases at this stage because you have so much responsibility behind you and so many dreams in front of you. Sometimes we get so overwhelmed with working that we can lose sight of our dreams.

I know that sounds crazy, but listen. Some people's dream is career and wealth. Some dreams are for family and comfort. But are either of these *your* dreams? You can be in such pursuit of your career that you neglect your family. Or you can be so focused on the responsibilities of the family and making their lives and dreams come true that you forget about your own dreams.

Again we find ourselves asking the questions, what am I doing, and where am I going? Many times we suffer from the overpursuit of other people's dreams! The career you pursue is what others say is a good career. It can also be what others say a good, strong family looks like. What do you say? This is where we have to go back and evaluate our foundations. It's the foundations or relationships that will keep you on the right course. This is the prime of your life, and you must be on the right track at this point. If you are not on the right track, you need to find that right track This is when your hard work needs to count for something.

> *"I must work the works of him that sent me, while it is day: the night cometh, when no man can work" (Jn 9:4 KJV).*

This passage is also talking about the stages of life.

When you're younger and have the strength and energy to work, then work. The day and time will come where you cannot work. The results of your work now have to be able to last far beyond what you can see right now. Your life depends on it.

If where you are spending your time and effort is not going to support you to and through the next stages of life, you need to reevaluate where you're spending your effort. Don't try to do this alone. Get some guidance and help in evaluating what you want to do. Figure out if what you want will sustain and support you. Because how you proceed from this point forward can determine how those in your domain will go. Many times the success of the people in our domain is directly related to the foundations we've built for them.

If you have not done so, this is a good time to establish the habit of a prayer. I don't mean just getting on your knees to tell God about everything going on in your life. And don't just tell God about all your troubles and needs. He already knows that. How about you use prayer to establish or reestablish a relationship with Him? Then learn to listen for direction. With all the distractions and busyness, this can be the hardest thing for men to do. It's something that you have to be very deliberate about and work at. But when you do, you'll begin to see the blueprints for where He's taking you.

Maturity (fifty-five to sixty-four):
And you thought you were mature at twenty-one, thirty, forty, and even fifty. Life has a way of normalizing your perspective. At this point in your life, you should be able to see so much more clearly. By this time, you should be who you are, and that should be a blessing to

everything you touch. We realize how precious the seasons of life really are. We have now numbered our days. Our mortality is before us, and our concerns in life at this point are our health and our legacies. What have I done that will leave an impression that I will be remembered for? What is my contribution to my domain and society? How much more can I get done with the time I have left? "So teach us to number our days, that we may apply our hearts unto wisdom" (Ps 90:12 KJV).

My statement at this point is that I know I'm not done yet. At this point, we should be in control of our resources. So how can we use our resources for the Lord? If there is ever a time for us to be significant, now is the time. Later, when we explore our purposes a little closer, we should be able to identify where we can make a difference by using our resources like time, money, wisdom, business, and community connections. What can we do to contribute to our fellow man?

They say that men have a season kind of like women's menopause. But I say it's "men-o-pause." This is when have to realize that we can't physically do the things we did in the past. You wake up in the morning to get out of bed much more slowly than you want to. You probably hear some bones cracking and feel a little pain over here and a little pain over there. You have to stretch a little bit before you get those first steps in. And that first step or two isn't quite as fast as the next few. Yes, you're reminded of your age almost every morning when you wake up.

As our health becomes more and more of a concern, there is one thing for sure that we need to do: *go to the doctor!* Men have a reputation for refusing to go to the doctor to get checkups. Men feel so violated when the doctor intrudes our innermost being. Women are used to it. Plus, some guys say, "Why should I go pay the doctor for some bad news?" Let me tell you, there are many men that didn't live to regret it! They might have gone too late or not at all.

A number of years ago, I put together a men's retreat. One of the speakers was Dr. Ronald Rembert. He discussed the "Five Numbers You Should Know for Men's Health." This was very eye opening for the men. It may have even saved someone's life. I know I went to the doctor after his talk.

Here are Dr. Rembert's notes:
Five Numbers You Should Know for Men's Health
(© 2010 by Ronald Rembert Jr. MD)

1) Blood Pressure (should be around 120/80 mm Hg. Above 140/90 is considered high blood pressure/ hypertension)

2) Cholesterol (Total-should be less than 200 mg/dL, LDL {bad cholesterol}-should be less than 130 and less than 100 if you have diabetes, hypertension or other diseases that increase your risk for stroke and heart attack, HDL {good cholesterol}-should be above 40 and above 60 decreases your risk of heart attacks and Triglycerides {a type of fat found in plants and animal fats and that our bodies make for energy}-should be less than 150)

3) Prostatic Serum Antigen (for men 50 and above or sooner if there is a family history)-should be less than

4.0 ng/dL and can be elevated in prostate cancer, prostatic enlargement from aging and in infections in the prostate.

4) Blood glucose (Fasting and 2 hour post-prandial {post-eating} blood sugar)-fasting blood sugar should be less than 125 mg/dL and post-eating blood sugar should be less than 200 mg/dL. Diabetes is diagnoses above those numbers.

5) Body Mass Index (this is a measurement of your weight vs. your height used to determine if someone is a normal weight for their height, overweight or obese {fat})-below 18.5 is considered underweight, 18.5-25 is considered normal weight, 26-30 is considered overweight and above 30 is considered obese {fat}. It is calculated by taking your weight in pounds X 703 and dividing that number by your height in inches squared: (Weight in pounds X 703)÷{(Height in inches)X(Height in inches)}.

Many men are facing retirement. This can be quite a devastating reality for some. You surely have to consider what will happen to the domain that depends on your support. I definitely recommend using professional planning for the next stages of your life. But what this also tells us is that the older you get, the less room for mistakes you can afford to make, because you have less time to recover from them. Selah!

Some people move to a better climate to suit their physical stresses. For most, that's a tough decision, unless you plan for it many years in advance, since you have to consider finances, family, and service providers— people like your doctors, dentists, bankers, and lawyers, and then there's the family, especially the grandkids. These are all things to be considered at this time of life.

Part of our experience is seeing an accelerated rate of our family and peers that have left us or are leaving us. We've been to way too many funerals and hospitals. We know enough to understand that tomorrow is not promised to us. We really don't know what's in store for us. Life really becomes day to day. You hope and pray for health and long life, but the longer you live, the more you're convinced that we need God more than ever.

The next question is, what can I do to revitalize my life? What will move me from success to significance? Some people, like myself, use this time as an opportunity to transition to a new livelihood. For me, it's going to be more teaching and coaching. For some it may be to become more of a sportsman, like taking up fishing and hunting. Maybe some want to do more in the community or church. Mission work is very rewarding to you and many others. Maybe it's a time to find your "Alaska."

What Is Your Alaska?
I call it that because many men have what some people call a "bucket list." Personally I don't like that term; it has such finality to it. Every man should have something different that he would like to do or try. I don't mean that midlife crisis stuff! I'm talking about something you've seen or thought you would enjoy, for no other reason than "just because."

My dad always had a dream about going deep-sea fishing—going for the big ones. He grew up in Mississippi, so fishing was like second nature to him.

But because of his work and his massive responsibility, he only went fishing a few times that I can remember. Well, there came a point in his life that he and some friends—another pastor and a mortician (of all people)—decided to take a trip to Alaska and hire a charter boat and crew. You know, one of the big fishing boats where you have to buckle down in the seat, and the fishing rod is bolted down to the deck with a big crank on it. Yeah, he was living.

They caught some pretty large fish. They caught salmon and halibut from about sixty to ninety pounds. They were so big that in order to kill them, he said they shot them with a .22 caliber gun. Needless to say, this was the trip of a lifetime for him. All I can say is he talked about it until the time when he couldn't talk anymore. For the first time in my life, I saw a happiness in him like I've never seen before. He was at peace. Guess what, now I want to take a trip to Alaska. I'm not the fisherman he was, so I won't be renting a charter, but I want to see the beauty and handiwork of God in that part of the world.

If you have not found your Alaska by the time you're in this age group, it's time for you to find someplace you want to see or something you want to do. This is one time when I really agree with the hats and t-shirts I see some of the kids wearing that say *YOLO*, meaning "you only live once."

Senior Citizen (sixty-five to seventy-nine):
We usually call this age group "seasoned," because most people I know in this age range know more than anyone in the world. They've experienced or have seen it all. Well, not quite. It's pretty hard to relate to young

people in this fast-paced cyber, cloud, agile, technical world we live in. It's moving at such a fast pace that most people in this age range give up trying to understand it, catch up to it, or even try to relate to it. The shame is that those in that youth category are not even mindful of the desires or importance of this group.

But what this age group does have is wisdom and experience that goes way beyond what younger people experience. This experience can be articulated in what I call philosophies of life, which are applicable at all ages. Senior citizens may not have to experience this fast-paced life of get it done quick, fast, and in a hurry, but I'd bet they can tell you principles that if applied, can propel you beyond any place you think you can go.

One thing they know for sure is what is important in life. They have a keen sense of neglected relationships and developmental patterns and being able to see pitfalls we may be headed toward. The concerns they have in life, most of us have never even considered.

The concerns for health at this point are foremost in the minds of senior citizens, because your health is usually an indicator of their longevity. Guess what. It's an indicator of your longevity at every age. Many people's health is directly related to their finances. Studies have shown that wealthy people are more conscious of their health and have better access to better health care, which results in fewer concerns and issues of health.

Speaking of finances, people who are what I call independently wealthy—meaning they don't need to look for income, and they probably have multiple streams of income—probably have all the support they need. But in this day and age, that is a small percentage of people. Others use a term that most young people are not used to: fixed income! This opens a big can of worms. I won't go into it, but a part of the reason I'm writing this is that I hear the voice of my seniors telling us that whatever you're going to do in life, do it quickly, because time is running out.

As we age, our perspective changes. Can't you see where people in younger stages are at a little better than they can? Well, how about establishing a relationship with someone outside of your stage in life? It should be bidirectional. You should have relationships with people already in the next stage of life where you're going. They probably can identify and help you through your discombobulated transition period. Hmm, I like that word, *discombobulated* (sorry, ADD kicking in). How about helping the generation before you? Helping them navigate through life? If we don't establish these relationships, it harms our society and our future.

From a spiritual perspective, this is usually the wealthiest, healthiest, and most productive age group. Why? Because as we age, our mortality is right before us, and we get closer to God. We also learn that it really is God in control. People in this age group have seen many people come and go—many family members, business, hopes, and dreams, all of which can vanish like fleeting bubbles. One thing for sure is that our senior citizens pray. I think the older we get, the more time we spend in prayer. Mom says, "I can do more on my knees than in any board room or any plans you or I might have." I think this is a lesson we need to learn from senior citizens.

Older men seem to become the silent generation. We need you to speak up. Younger men, we need you to engage. I have always found men of the generation before me to communicate with. I learn from them: my uncles, the men in the church, the men in the neighborhood. I have always found guys of the next generation to learn from and to teach or impart wisdom to me. Young and old, who are you connecting with?

I remember a long time ago, my mother pointed me to a Bible passage that has become one of my favorite passages in the Bible. It's by a man named King Solomon, son of King David—you know the one, the giant slayer. God allowed King Solomon to have more of anything any man could possibly desire. If you can imagine it, he had it. Money, wisdom, women galore; he had property, livestock, servants, even armies at his disposal; he literally had it all. After many trials and tribulations over life's mazes and telling us that all desires are but vanity, he summed up all of his experience, wisdom, and knowledge in the final passage he wrote to us, "Having heard everything, I have reached this conclusion: Fear God and keep his commandments, because this is the whole duty of man. For God will evaluate every deed, including every secret thing, whether good or evil" (Eccl 12:13–14 NET).

Dotage (eighty years and older):
At this stage in our lives, we've seen many friends and family pass on to eternity. We've seen some suffering and some grief like never before. Some men remain alert active senior citizens, but still need assistance living day to day. There are those that can rejoice in knowing that we've survived and come through so much in life. Here we value life more than we ever have

before, but we also have an appreciation and almost an anticipation of eternity. We don't usually think about our lives holistically. We think about where we are right now and maybe where we want to be in a few years. But how many of us think in terms of how we're going to end this thing. How many of us have what I call a real "exit strategy?" What are the conditions of our health, our wealth, and most importantly, our relationships? Each of these are so important to the quality of life as we live out our last stages of life.

The scripture that says "work while it is day" also speaks about the night, "when no man can work." It didn't say no man *should* work, it says "no man *can* work": "I must work the works of him that sent me, while it is day: the night cometh, when no man can work" (Jn 9:4 KJV).

There is a point in your life where you cannot work or build or do much of anything. This is when you have to depend on others for your care and well-being.

When I spoke of building foundations in an earlier chapter and your greatest investment being in yourself, I was also talking about the time when you will have to stand on those foundations and withdraw from those investments to sustain you. Those investments in God, family, church, and personal wealth will determine the quality of your life in your latter days.

Consider these options based on your self-investments. First imagine being sick and old, barely able to care for yourself, and having no real relationships with anyone to help care for you. You are financially strapped and unable to buy medicine and the things you need to live.

The other option is to have built a great family filled with love and prosperity and having established long-standing relationships with family, church, friends, business partners, and community.

I imagine like in old movies where an old guy is in bed in his last dying days, and he has this huge house, with a big, winding staircase going up to his room. There he lies in a large, four-poster canopy bed in a sleeping gown and sleeping cap. His wife, children, and a host of grandchildren are gathered around his bed. His private nurse gives him his medicine as the doctor arrives up the stairs. The doctor has his little black bag and stethoscope and is now checking the man's lungs.

Which of the two cases reflects a successfully built foundation and evidence of time well invested? This is what I mean when I say you eventually have to stand on the foundations you've built.

When you have a solid foundation, you can develop a solid exit strategy. In that I mean preparing for the inevitable—making preparation so that your exit will not cause turmoil, strife, and burden on the ones you leave behind. I've seen families curse the day men were born because of the way the men died.

In my father's death, he taught me one of my greatest lessons about living. He had an impeccable exit strategy. He totally prepared the world he lived in for his own exit. As a father, he prepared for the family's financial support. He financed his own funeral and burial expenses. As a pastor, he established my older brother as his successor and installed him as pastor. As a bishop, he saw to it that three men were elevated to cover his ecclesiastical responsibilities. There was left no question as to his wishes after he left us. His work was complete, but his legacy is alive and well. He left the world a better place because he was here. For that, I respectfully say, thank you, Bishop Dr. Samuel S. McCarthy!

If you love your family and want to be well remembered, have a well-established exit strategy so your memory will not be tainted by leaving behind hardships and pain. Even better than having an exit plan is having an established relationship with God Himself. With a well-established exit plan, you prepare for quality of life *before* leaving earth, but with an established relationship with God, you prepare for quality of life *after* leaving earth. "But on the judgment day, fire will reveal what kind of work each builder has done. The fire will show if a person's work has any value" (1 Cor 3:13 NIV).

Afterlife:
Even for those that may not believe in the afterlife, guess what? After you die, even if we are all wrong and there's nothing there, it's still "after life!" OK, let me confess. I do believe in the afterlife. It's really "after life *on earth*," because we continue to live—it's just a matter of where. To live beneath your means, meaning life without Christ, is death. By this point, I hope you've prayed that prayer earlier in the book or even taken the challenge to ask Jesus to show Himself to you. If you did, you should be able to recognize Him in your life. I believe the Bible when it quotes Jesus as saying, "I am the way, the truth, and the life. No one comes to the Father except through Me" (Jn 14:6 NKJV).

In 1998, my mother wrote a memo to my sister Joreece;

this was four years before Joreece passed in 2003. Joreece sent the memo in an e-mail to our other siblings. Another sister on the e-mail list, Lorna, passed in 2008. Here is the e-mail that Joreece sent. I thought it was so appropriate to end this chapter.

```
Author:  Joreece Mackie <jmackie@muchlaw.com> at INTERNET
Date:    10/22/98  10:18 AM
Priority: Normal
Receipt Requested
TO: "'DIONDEBRA@AOL.COM'" <DIONDEBRA@AOL.COM> at INTERNET,
    Ellis C McCarthy at FNBC_CIB_NSGO_05,
    "'Lorna.Townes@stpaul.com'" <Lorna.Townes@stpaul.com> at INTERNET,
    "'YARBROUGHS@NAPERVILLE.IL.US'" <YARBROUGHS@NAPERVILLE.IL.US> at INTERNET,
    "'Joreece@aol.com'" <Joreece@AOL.COM> at INTERNET
Subject: No subject given

October 22, 1998
Thursday, 6:00 a.m.
Written by Mother Omega McCarthy

My Times Are In Thy Hand
Palsms 31:15

Life is so temporary.  No matter what we are going through, our marriage,
our children, our home, our job, whatever it is, it is all only a temporary
situation.  When it all passes, and time changes places with eternity, where
will you be?  None of the temporaries will mean a thing to you.

Time moves very swiftly.  Years go by very fast.  Look back over your life
and you will see what I mean.  Each phase has passed and gone.  Infancy,
childhood, teenage years, young  adult, middle age, and whatever stage you
are in, it will soon be over.

When you look back at your failures and your regrets you will be so sorry.
When you look back at your successes and your accomplishments and your walk
with God you will be so glad.

Make every minute from now on out count toward your eternal destination.
Remember to deal fairly with all your fellow men in every situation.  Time
is running swiftly.  Time is a temporary situation, eternity is forever.

My times are in thy hand.  Palsms 31:15

                    By:  Mother Omega McCarthy
```

I have read the Bible and believe every word of it. I've established a relationship with Jesus Christ. I have an internal witness of His presence and operation in my life. I have a relationship with Him. I believe that after my life is over, I will be with Him. I also believe if I do not have that relationship, I will be destined to spend eternity out of His presence in a place called hell. I'm not trying to convince you of this. I'm just declaring what I believe. Each individual has to decide for him or herself what he or she believes. There is life after death. It will be with Christ or without Christ.

-Eight-
PERSONAL GROWTH PROGRESSION

We've talked about the stages of life for men, identifying some of the conditions and transitions from stage to stage. But we all have what I call our own Personal Growth Progression (PGP).

One thing that is constant in our progressions from one stage to the next is change. We are constantly changing every day. Many times we fail to recognize the changes or the affect they have on our lives. If we looked at our lives' changes on one linear time line, we should be able to map major changes in our lives on that time line. When we get to the end of that line, will we have accomplished all of our hopes and dreams? More importantly, will we have accomplished the purpose for which God created us? Right now, your personal growth progression only goes as far as today. Tomorrow it will extend another day, and each day we live, it will extend further. Each day we have the opportunity to make decisions to get closer to our God-given purposes.

Your personal growth progression is mapped by the day-to-day decisions and events that shape your life. The events that bring about change in your life can have a positive or a negative effect. Some changes can even cause you to be stagnant, meaning that where you would be taking action or making progress, progress doesn't happen; things remain the same. Even then, change is going on; we're just not unaware of it. There are times when we reflect back and say, "Remember when this happened? If I had done X, I would have been Z." I think we've all had those moments. These events I'm talking about are what I call watershed moments—moments that shape our lives and that always seem to bring us to that proverbial fork in the road. Every time we have one of these watershed moments, we can mark it on our PGP as a positive step (+), a negative step (-), or just a period of stagnation (=). I call these progression points, because they mark changes or options in our lives' progressions.

Watershed moments are when we make certain decisions or when decisions are made for us. It can be when certain events occur in our lives and sometimes just by chance. There may be some events that we have no control over or decisions like what college to attend or what career path to take or even what girl to marry. It could even be something like, "Whew, man, I am *so* glad I didn't marry *that* girl!" Or let's say by chance you're responsible for ticket sales for the Portland Trailblazers basketball team in 1984! You're watching the NBA draft on TV, and you see your team just pass on drafting Michael Jordan! Think that decision affected the sales guy's PGP? And look at Michael Jordan and the rest of the Chicago Bulls' PGP. How did that work out for them? I think you get the point!

The PGP is just a perspective of where you are in your life right now. It's to evaluate how decisions and events in your life have affected you. It's not a way to make excuses for where you are but a chance to reflect on the things you had control of and things you didn't. A divorce has little to do with the kids, although kids sometimes carry the baggage of feeling like it's their fault. If that's you, trust me, it's not your fault, and you probably had very little to do with it. My mom had a sign on her refrigerator that said, "It's not what happens to you in life that matters, but how you handle those things is what matters." If we have a better perspective of things that happen to us or decisions that we face, we can have a better response and produce better results and put more plus signs on our PGPs.

The reason I came up with the PGP is to help with my future decisions and events. I wanted to look back at the events in my life so I could be more conscious of how those decisions affected me. Now I can be more aware of how my future decisions are going to affect my life and those around me before I make them. My PGP is also a measuring stick to see where I am in my hopes, dreams, and more importantly, my purpose. Take a PGP for yourself and reflect on your life history. A practical example of some of the things on my PGP is as follows:

When I was nine, my grandmother died. I say that was a minus (-). Why? Because I was her baby. She had me spoiled rotten. This was one of my first traumas in my life. In sixth grade I experienced bullying for the first time. I overcame it. I threw myself into my studies, which I felt did not come naturally, because I wanted to be on top of my class. I then suffered a setback when I had to miss a lot of school due to medical issues. I still ended up ranking third in my graduating class and was allowed to emcee the graduation; that was a plus. I didn't realize this would be the first experience that led to many years of being the pulpit conductor every Sunday and being the emcee for many special occasions in the church (more pluses). The sad part was that my dad was a preacher and public servant who was called to a previously scheduled ministry event and couldn't attend the graduation. And this was my proudest moment (-). In retrospect, no one knows how hard I worked for that honor. Why is this so significant? Because after years of struggle to perform and do my best, I always seem to come up short. Even failure in high school was an unexplainable shock to the system (-). Then in my later years, I was diagnosed with adult attention deficit disorder (ADD). Many years ago, that was not on anyone's radar yet. Imagine how that affected my life. It explained a lot of things. Well, actually being aware of it and managing it turned into a number of big pluses!

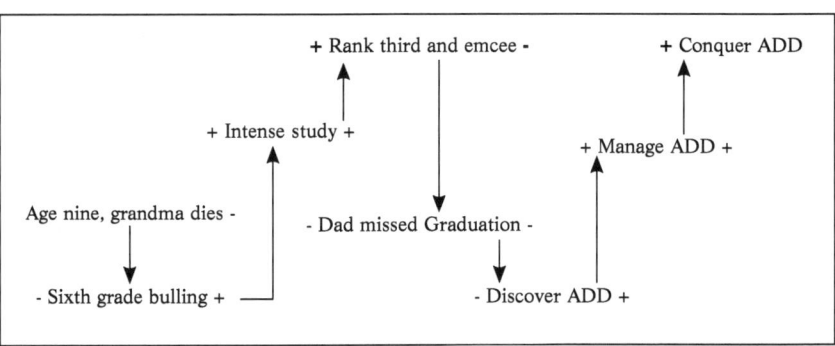

I could go on and on with many stories of successes and failures, but the point is that looking at my total PGP, I can see why I am where I am in life. I could have taken many paths, but God has brought me to the place where I am right now. And just like me, you have the opportunity to look at where you are and create many more pluses on your PGP. You can do so by the decisions that you make and how you handle the watershed moments in your life. Remember I said earlier that part of our responsibility as men is to be concerned with the health, wealth, and well-being for everyone in our domain? This has to be a major factor in our decision making.

Examine your life, and mark the changes in your life, or identify the points where there should have been change but wasn't. Now mark the age, year, or time when those things happen in your life with a plus, minus, or equal sign progression point. You'll have your PGP.

IDEAL GROWTH PROGRESSION

Just like we have a personal growth progression, I believe we have what I call an Ideal Growth Progression (IGP). I define this as the timeline for fulfilling your God-given purpose. It has progression points that we will have to face along the way. The PGP covered our timeline up to today. With the IGP, our timeline reflects our lives beyond today, all the way to the time of fulfilling or completing our purposes.

In order to draw this timeline, you would have to know your purpose. Imagine your IGP as though God himself drew your PGP through to the end of your life. The progression points on your IGP timeline from this day forward would be all pluses. When looking at our PGP, we can see the pluses. How many of those same points would be on the timeline of your IGP? But would we have the minuses? Doing this, I realized the progression points on the PGP and IGP are decisions we face every day. And we make these choices every day without knowing our true purpose. This is why our PGP would look so different than our IGP for the same time frame.

One thing we need to be aware of is the fact that we learn to make decisions from those around us or those that teach us. We learn our colors and ABCs from our moms; we learn that two plus two equals four from our teachers. When you make decisions, are they based on a learning model that seems right to you because you've seen it that way or learned it that way all your life? Did you learn it from your father or grandfather, did you learn it from someone you looked up to in the streets, or did you learn it from your peers? We should really think about major decisions independently of past influences. Be careful—I said past *influences*, which is different from our past experiences. Think about it.

Without knowing our purposes, we have to trust God. The symbol that ends up on every progression points comes down to hearing God and then deciding whether you're going to obey or disobey. Like I said in the chapter "On Purpose," the choices we make will either lead us *to* our purposes or draw us *away* from our purposes. We waste time with the baggage of ramifications and consequences. If you knew your purpose and were drawing your ideal growth progression from this point in your life forward, it would be much easier to navigate through life and make decisions!

MAKING DECISIONS ON PURPOSE
As we live, we constantly experience watershed moments to which we have to make a decisions or respond. Notice I didn't say *react*. A reaction is making a decision based on the current circumstances. Any decision made on current circumstances may only

accommodate the current situation and not our long-term purpose. Sometimes we have to make a short-term decision, but we have to make sure it only has a short term effect. I heard someone say it like this, "Don't make a permanent decision for a temporary situation." Our decisions need to be made *on purpose.*

So the goal here is to make decisions that align your personal growth progression with your ideal growth progression, just as God designed it. So when we hit the fork in the road, we can respond or make decisions based on the purpose that God has given us. Now we can have a different outlook where every decision (progression point) we come to will mark another step toward our goal. When we look behind us, our PGP will begin to take on a different shape. That's not to say we won't have minuses, but even those minuses will get us closer to our IGP. Sometimes the minuses are by design. Don't tell me you expected me to say you'll have smooth sailing with no bumps in the road. Wake up— you're not in a fairy tale. Of course there will be bumps in the road.

Even the bumps in the road can help equip you. They can actually be there to prevent you from having pitfalls. When our decisions are based on selfish gain or misaligned purpose, it can lead us in to a pitfall or trap that can take years to correct or get out of.

Sometimes those bumps in the road are for growth, and sometimes they are for you to stop and learn to help others grow. Like in ministry...now there's a thought...

I talked earlier about being stagnant. Stagnation in this sense is not without motion. If you are stagnant, that means you are not growing, but you are not regressing. It's OK if you have a minus that helps equip you or takes you on a detour or another path to your goal. But when you're stagnant, you are actually getting further from your goal by not progressing toward your goal. That is to say you now have less time to get there. If you stay stagnant too long, you'll fall into what I call *the comfort zone!*

I've seen where guys have a pretty good track record at their jobs. Their finances are situated well enough to be very comfortable. Their wife is pretty content with the family's lifestyle. These guys can pretty much do whatever they want: drive a decent car and have a decent home, and their kids doing pretty well. All they have to do is ride it out, save a little money, and ride off into the sunset of life without a struggle or a care. People like this are in a comfort zone.

So what if you never become "significant?" What if no one benefits from your knowledge and experience? You might leave a tip here and there, so "I'm good," you say. Let me tell you: I do not want to leave this earth comfortably but with my purpose unfulfilled! My desire is to be comfortable because I'm enjoying the benefits God has afforded me for being more than significant and for doing His will, *which is what I'm designed to do.*

The bottom line is this. When we have our relationships in order, which gives us a solid foundation to stand on, we can look at every fork in the road as an opportunity to get closer to God and closer to our purposes. We have to live intentionally so that the decisions we make will be *deliberate,* and they MUST be made *on purpose!*

"I am not a product of my circumstances; I am a product of my decisions."

~ Steven Covey

I want to leave you with a motto for you to ponder. God gave me this many years ago to contemplate for myself. After years of trying to understand it, I'm now beginning to figure out how to live by this motto.

"Don't let your situations and circumstances dictate your decisions. Instead, make your decisions dictate your circumstances and situations!"

-Nine-
FINDING GOD'S PURPOSE

Sometimes we can be heavily in pursuit of something that we really desire and long to attain, but it seems the more we go after it and the more we pursue it, the further away it seems. It may be that we have it right in our hands, but we still struggle with it. We might have what we call a passion for it—but is it a divine passion given by God, or is it just something we really deeply desire? When we are in pursuit of our desires year after year, we have to ask ourselves, do I have a *misaligned passion*?

I believe that God gives us a *divine passion*. That's a passion that God has placed in us from birth and that is uniquely designed specifically for each one of us. Sometimes we don't connect to our divine passion right away and sometimes not for many years, even if we don't recognize it or identify with it for some time. But when we find it and recognize it, there's no doubt that this is what we were made to do. There is no greater pursuit that can satisfy us. It comes naturally.

When you are working in your divine passion, things come easily. Your aptitude for that thing comes easily as well. Your abilities excel rapidly. When you become educated in the thing that is your passion, your development and productivity progress far beyond your peers' education or experience. Some people have a knack for their passion is. Then you run in to people who are trying what you're doing, and we find that they may just be working in a misaligned passion. In other words, you have a knack for it, and they have a "NAC." That's an acronym for "not a clue!"

LET'S FIND OUR PASSIONS

What is it that you love to do or really wish you could be doing? Better yet, what gives you peace or a sense of joy when you hear it or talk about it? Many of us don't immediately recognize our passions, but believe me, it's there.

Think about it. When was the last time you thought about what you really want to do? Maybe you've never known or have never thought about having that feeling of satisfaction or fulfillment in an activity. Whether you're already doing what you love or you're looking for that one thing to love, answer this: what is the skill that you really wish you had or had more of? I'm not talking about just something that you're good at but the one thing that could give you a sense of satisfaction. Now think of why you would want that skill. If you can answer this question, hold that thought. Write it down, and save it for future reference.

When we can't identify our passions, maybe we can identify our first love or a passion we had earlier in life. It seems the older we get, the more the *issues of life* get in our way. Our attention to everyday life can make us forget or not think about what we really love doing.

One morning my wife and I were talking about one of her passions, and it seemed like God was saying to me, "Ask her what her first love was." When I say "first love," I don't mean the first person she fell in love with. But when you were young and making discoveries in life, can you identify what you were most attracted to or loved doing or being involved with? What was it that you took great joy in thinking about, being around, or even participating in? After I asked my wife this question, it dawned on me as she was speaking that her first love was directly linked to what she now considers her current passion. Now, think about it: what was your first love?

If you were able to write down the answer to the question from the previous paragraph about what skill you wanted or why you would want that skill, examine it and compare it to what I described as your first love. See if you can find any links between your first love and that skill you wrote down. Maybe compare the first love to the reason you want that new skill. By examining these facts, you may be able to see a connection to your underlying passion that you do not currently recognize.

In some cases, maybe you have not had the opportunity to have a wide range of experiences and never came across anything that struck that "passion nerve." Let's do a little self-evaluation. See if you can determine if there's anything you would have liked to try, just to experience it.

I believe all of us can look back and find missed opportunities in our lives. But I also believe we miss opportunities every day to do something different or to try something we've never tried or experienced before.

Even if you know what your passion is and you're actively pursuing it, there are always things we can do to enhance our experiences.

I don't know what your divine passion is, but the first step to finding it is going to take some time, some prayer, and some meditation. Sometimes we have to stop what we are doing to figure out what we are doing! There's an old cliché that says, "If you do what you love, you will never work a day in your life." What this actually means is that when your work is what you love or are passionate about, you don't consider it work at all. You'll be accomplishing something that is important to you and important to others.

Years ago, I once heard a saying from one of Dr. Miles Monroe's teachings that really stuck with me. He said, "If you want to know the purpose of a thing, ask the creator of that thing." Only the creator can know the purpose for which he created the object. You can't ask a machine like a car, a tool, like forklift, "Why were you created?" You'd have to ask the maker of that machine or that tool why it was created. Some things are a lot more obvious than others. So what about you? Why were you created?

God Himself created you! He knew who you would be you before He ever created you. He knew you before you were even born (Ps 139:13–16). He also had a plan for you, just like He had for Jeremiah (Jer 1:5).

> *"You made all the delicate inner parts of my body and knit me together in my mother's womb. Thank you for making me so wonderfully complex! Your workmanship is marvelous—*

how well I know it. You watched me as I was being formed in utter seclusion, as I was woven together in the dark of the womb. You saw me before I was born. Every day of my life was recorded in your book. Every moment was laid out before a single day had passed" (Ps 139:13–16 NLT).

"I knew you before I formed you in your mother's womb. Before you were born I set you apart and appointed you as my prophet to the nations" (Jer 1:5 NLT).

At some point in his life, every man asks himself the age old question, "Why was I created; what is the purpose of my life?" Well, I believe to answer that question is that you have to ask your Creator. That's why I say it takes time, prayer, and meditation to find your passion. Finding your passion leads to finding your divine purpose. Once you find your purpose, you can start taking action, making decisions, and doing things deliberately and *on purpose.*

YOUR PURPOSE PURSUES YOU
One thing that has a profound effect on us as men is the fact that while we are in pursuit of self-satisfaction and the pursuit of purpose, we miss one major fact: while you are pursuing purpose, purpose is pursuing you. So many options and opportunities come your way when you have to make direction-changing decisions. They say opportunity only knocks once, but I don't believe that. As many times as I've failed to seize opportunities, God always find a way to send me another one. It's the ones I capitalize on where I find any success.

When God opens certain doors of opportunity, this is purpose pursuing you. We have to recognize when a watershed moment is upon us and is about to change the course of our lives. We have to hear God, trust God, seize the moment, and let the God-given purpose come alive to accomplish what He needs from us and in us. This is obeying God.

When I started obeying the voice inside of me telling me to write a book, things started happening that I never imagined. I thought that voice in my head was just my wife pushing me (OK, God was using her too), but it was God pushing me to my purpose. This is an example *of making my decisions dictate my circumstances!*

Nature, which is everything that God created, cooperates with God. So when your divine purpose is tapped into, everything that is supposed to support you doing what you were created to do *is going to cooperate with you!*

> *"For the creation waits in eager expectation for the children of God to be revealed" (Rom 8:19 NIV).*

I interpret this passage to mean that everything in creation is expecting you and your God-given purpose to be identified. Why? So it can cooperate with you and your purpose in fulfilling the plan of God. I know this can be considered a loose interpretation. I am not talking about a doctrine of superhuman beings, but the principle is about being aligned with God's will for your life, which is our role in God's redemptive plan. That's not to say there will not be obstacles or opposition. You must be aligned and watch what God does.

Everything God created is obedient to its purpose—except *man!* Everything else is submitted to its purpose; the only thing it can do is fulfill its purpose or the reason it was created. Man is the only creature that has a choice in the matter.

Think about it. No one has to tell the rooster when to get up and go to work and start crowing! Hmm. No one has to tell the leaves when to change colors or when to fall. No one has to convince the tide to ebb and flow! Bees know how and when to make honey!

But all of creation is waiting to see who the sons of God really are. How will creation know who the real sons of God are? I believe that just like no one has to tell creation its role, no will have to tell a man when he is operating in his purpose.

We have a choice. God gave us free will. We are the only creation that God made to which He gave a choice about whether we will obey and follow our purposes. That's how much He loves us. The power to choose is so great that by giving us free will, He allows us to risk our eternal future just so we can have a choice. Remember, the choice is to obey or disobey—obedience to God and our internal God-given passions will lead us to our purposes.

> "The subconscious mind may be likened to a magnet, and when it has been vitalized and thoroughly saturated with any definite purpose, it has a decided tendency to attract all that is necessary for the fulfillment of that purpose."
> ~ Napoleon Hill

Thinking

If you think you are beaten, you are
If you think you dare not, you don't,
If you like to win, but you think you can't
It is almost certain you won't.

If you think you'll lose, you're lost
For out of the world we find,
Success begins with a fellow's will
It's all in the state of mind.

If you think you are outclassed, you are
You've got to think high to rise,
You've got to be sure of yourself before
You can ever win a prize.

Life's battles don't always go
To the stronger or faster man,
But soon or late the man who wins
Is the man WHO THINKS HE CAN!

~ Walter D. Wintle ~

-Ten-
BLUEPRINT FOR FULFILLING GOD'S PURPOSE

There is no magic bullet to finding God's purpose. You may never even know your full purpose until it's fulfilled. As a matter of fact, you may not even know when it is fulfilled. It could be that your purpose is to plant a seed—a seed that will grow into something you can't even imagine. Do you think Ben Franklin or Thomas Edison ever imagined what the world would become from their roles in using electricity and discovering what it can do? From their initial work, we have everything from a light bulb to planetary exploration. Pablo Picasso probably never imagined his work would command millions of dollars! Again, this is another reason I've said that our greatest pursuit has to be God Himself. So what's the big deal with finding your passion and man's desire to find his purpose?

"Your purpose is hidden in your journey"

There are many books, preached messages, videos, and classes galore on finding purpose. So after spending so much time on creating a personal growth progression and looking for our passions, you mean we won't even tie it all together and have the ultimate answer to our purpose? Well, to be honest, I cannot tell you your purpose. I am more concerned with fulfilling my purpose than finding it! I do not want to leave this earth with unfulfilled purpose or with assignments from God still on the table. I intend to fulfill every assignment God has given me.

When I talked about your purpose pursuing you, that process is like a finding a path that is carved out before you to find the way to your destination. You have no idea where that destination is, but you are challenged to get there, kind of like the starship Enterprise, going where no man has gone before. You've taken off into space but have no idea where you're going to land or no clue what adventures you're going to encounter on the way. If we knew exactly where God was taking us, we'd surely put up billboard telling the world where we're going and get an airplane to write it in the sky. But I don't think he wants us to do that. He just wants us to fulfill it. What happens along the way happens. That doesn't mean "Hakuna Matata," the song from the *Lion King*, was right. Sometimes we think, "If I could only know my purpose, then I would start singing, 'It means no worries for the rest of your days. It's our problem-free philosophy: hakuna matata.'" Believe me, it doesn't work like that.

So here's the question. How can we know what our ideal growth progression is supposed to look like, how can we make decisions on purpose, and how can we find the path to our purposes if we don't know what the destination is?

Well, I'm glad you asked. The goal is not necessarily to just find our purposes but to fulfill them. The path to fulfilling your purpose starts with your pursuit of God. That begins with the first foundation, which is building a relationship with God through praying and studying the word of God, which is the Holy Bible. As you build the relationship, learn to hear and trust God's voice. I remember many years ago, Christians used to ask us if we knew God's telephone number. They'd tell us it was Jeremiah 33:3, where God said, "Call to me, and I will answer you, and show you great and mighty things, which you do not know" (Jer 33:3 NKJV).

In your prayer time, ask God to help you identify the passions that He has placed in you. Ask Him to awaken that thing that you just can't find peace without. I believe if you are serious, God will direct you and awaken that passion. Why is that passion so important? Because if you begin to apply yourself to your passion and pursue accomplishing the very thing that's inside of you, you will began to feel a drive in you that won't let go. You will be so conscious of it that you'll start wondering why this thing has been on your mind so much. Your passion will become your desire.

Why do I say that? Look at the full definition of desire: "Conscious impulse toward something that promises enjoyment or satisfaction in its attainment." Your passion becomes your quest for attaining satisfaction in your life's accomplishments. Applying yourself to your passion will drive you to figuring out a way to make it happen. Your desire will cause your continual pursuit of that thing you've become passionate about. It will give you the strength to keep going after it.

"You grew weary in your search, but you never gave up. Desire gave you renewed strength, and you did not grow weary" (Is 57:10 NLT).

But be careful here. Many false opportunities can show up. You can be so in pursuit of your desire that you can be misguided. That's why it's so important to continuously stay in prayer and keep hearing God's voice. I can't emphasize enough how important it is to adhere to Proverbs 3:5, where it tells us to acknowledge God, and He will direct our paths! There is spiritual opposition to fulfilling God's purpose for you. Let alone fulfilling it—the opposition doesn't even want you to find the path that leads to it.

This is why consecration is so important. To be consecrated means to be dedicated for God's purpose. It means to be very deliberate in setting aside other pursuits for the purpose of being close to God, being led by God, and being available for God. Having the desire to build a relationship with Him sometimes that means spending time alone meditating on His word and being in His presence. This is where you'll truly find your divine passion.

As you apply yourself to your passion, a mysterious thing will begin to happen. You will start having more insight into your efforts. Remember, I said when you're operating in your divine passion, things will *come* easy for you. What I mean is you will receive insight and direction. That doesn't mean it will *be* easy. Things may not happen immediately, because all things have to happen in God's timing. You may have to break through some barriers. But through it all, at some point you'll be able to accomplish more than the effort you put forth. Or things will seem to fall into place for you. When you're working in your divine passion, you seem to have skills or gifting in a particular area. Your extraordinary skills are part of your gifting. I believe everyone has gifts from God. These gifts are to be used to help you excel in life and in God. When your skills or gifts are dedicated to doing God's will, new doors of opportunity will be open to you.

Again, be careful. When you have selfish goals or want success for the wrong reasons, there will also be opportunity available—opportunity for disobedience to God's will and purpose for your life. This may get you fame or fortune but will never lead to God's purpose for your life. You will find those consequences and ramifications somewhere along the way. I can point you to many celebrities that have paid the price of misguided purpose that ends up in tragedy, their death, or even the death of loved ones, all of which may come at an early age or prematurely.

So we have to trust God to know which opportunities to pursue. When we line up our desires with His desires, we will have a peace about which opportunities to pursue. We have to let the peace of God rule our hearts. When we do that, we can realize the Bible verse that says He will give us the desires of our heart (Psa 37:4 KJV). The key is aligning your heart with God's heart. You have to find your opportunity and trust the peace of God to be able to say yes!

YOUR GIFT MAKES ROOM FOR YOU
There's a passage in the Bible that I've always questioned. It says, "A man's gift makes room for him, and brings him before great men" (Prv 18:16).

A gift in this passage means bringing someone a gift or a present will gain you access to great men of influence. It's kind of like paying to get into the door or in front of the line. But I believe the general use of this passage also means the gifts or skills that you have will open doors for you also. You can look at the lives of people we consider great or exceptional that are well known, and you'll see people whose skills and talent have opened doors for them. Look at your favorite actor, author, athlete, musician, or singer. These people having skills and having doors opened for them does not mean they did not put in the work and the effort to be great.

How does that apply to you and your pursuit of fulfilling God's purpose for you? I asked God this question: "How does it work that your gifts make room for you?" Of course, He didn't answer right away. So I kept this question in mind as I read and studied the scriptures. One day after I was praying, a scripture popped in my head. I wasn't thinking about it. In fact, when the scripture came to me, it was a chapter and verse. I was familiar with the area, but couldn't think of what this verse said. It was Ephesians 4:7: "But unto every one of us is given grace according to the measure of the gift of Christ" (Eph 4:7 KJV).

This tells me that my gift is from Christ, and with it comes *grace*, which is God's favor. It's the grace on your gifting that opens doors and bring you before great men, just like you've given someone a payment or something they desire to get ahead or to get close to a person of influence. Better yet, having God's grace is more like *someone else* pay for that gift or desired thing that's gets you access to great men of influence. I can get into a web of theological discussions on what the writer, the apostle Paul, was telling us, but the simple answer that I believe God was trying to tell me is this: when I apply myself to the gifts that He gave me, doors will be opened by the grace of God on my life and on my gifting. This speaks to our natural gifts but more so to our spiritual gifts. When Christ gave His own life, He gave us spiritual gifts.

We have natural giftings, which we can see in the special skills we have—like we've discussed—but each of us also has spiritual gifts. These are spiritual skills, so to speak, that work by God's power to fulfill God's purpose through us. The need to understand these gifts is why we need to be in a good Bible-teaching church. At the church I attend, we have a class for members called "Discovering and Using Your Spiritual Gifts." You can find some of these gifts in the Bible in 1 Corinthians 12. Please be advised that these gifts need to be identified, properly trained, and exercised so that God can use them for His purpose.

Our spiritual gifts are developed similarly to our natural gifts. Take our faith as an example. We have what I like to call "faith aerobics." For many years, when someone is facing a challenging situation, I've heard people say, "You just need to exercise your faith" or "You need to build up your faith." I would question, how do you do that? Well, like in aerobics, you're exercising to build muscle and strength. There comes a time when you have to use that strength. If a bookshelf or something heavy falls on you, you have to apply the muscle that's been built up. So if I have a headache, I exercise my faith to be healed. If I need favor for something, I exercise my faith. I exercise my faith to receive the promises of God that I read about in the Bible. But if there is a critical situation, I have to *apply* my faith. If the doctor gives you a bad report, sometimes it's not time to exercise faith—it's time to apply it! We need to have built up our strength in knowing that faith comes by hearing the word of God.

Our spiritual gifts need to be exercised and developed. In the process of using our natural gifts and our spiritual gifts, doors will be opened. Why? So that the will of God for your life and your purpose can be fulfilled. In time you'll began to see and understand the scriptures that tells us how creation is cooperating with our purposes. We'll know that our purposes are pursuing us. It's like being chased by a dream that has to be brought to life. As you begin to walk through those open doors, some of which have to be knocked down, Roman 8:24 will come alive in you: "And we know that all things work together for good to them that love God, to them who are the called according to his purpose" (Rom 8:28 KJV).

I consider this one of the scriptures most used out of context. It doesn't apply to everything or everybody. It's for those who are called according to God's purpose. Remember, it's not your purpose, it's your role in God's plan, and He is there to help you fulfill it!

In summary, there's no silver bullet, but there is a way to find the path to fulfilling your purpose. This is not the only way, but if you haven't found your way, you can start with this one: find your God-given passion deep inside of you. Pray and ask God to help you identify that pure passion inside of you. I know it's there. Learn and apply yourself to that passion. In doing so, you'll find your natural gifts and your spiritual gifts. The grace of God on your gifts will began to make room for you and bring you before great men. In time, you'll see that the Bible is true and that all things really do work together for your good, the called of God, according to *His purpose!* But remember, it starts with *love.*

> *"And we know that all things work together for good to them that love God, to them who are the called according to his purpose" (Rom 8:28 KJV, emphasis mine).*

Our purpose is not for our own achievements or for our own glory. We are a small piece—but a very important piece—of God's plan for humanity. Christ came that none should be lost. We have a part to play in that. As we follow the path, His will shall be done.

> "Aspiration is greater than realization, because it keeps us eternally climbing upward toward some unattained goal."
>
> ~ Napoleon Hill

Eleven

IT'S MY SEASON
IT'S MY TIME

"To every thing there is a season, and a time to every purpose under the heaven" (Eccl 3:1 KJV).

Whenever I hear this scripture preached, it is always connected to the next seven verses behind it. It seems to always be preached at funerals, when someone wanted to impress upon us that there is a time to die; that always irritated me. Because I know about the tradition of the Hebrews writing in the contrast and comparison style, I wanted someone to also identify when it was time to live. Why do they only tell me when it's time to die, and I'm already at a funeral? Duhhh! OK, sorry for the rant, but as you see—I'm irritated! Now, back to my topic.

What I really wanted to point out is that the first verse of Ecclesiastes does apply to the things listed in the seven verses behind it, but God is showing me that it also applies to everything that God has created, including you and me. As we've seen in previous chapters in this book, we all have a divine purpose.

Seasons go come and go, in and out. I've always been

told there are many seasons in life. When we examine the life cycles of men, we can see the seasons as they come and go. There are seasons for everything listed in Ecclesiastes 3:2–8. But how about looking at the time for *your* purpose?

When the verse says there is a time to every purpose under the sun, I realize that I have a purpose, and there is a time for *my* purpose. When that time comes, the purpose that I was created for will produce what I was created to produce. God will take all the teachings I have learned, all the gifting that I've received, all the grace He has given me, and all of His anointing He has placed in me and use it all to produce what He created me to accomplish. At that point in time, I will be fulfilling God's purpose of my life, though Him! It may be but a moment or can be for a season. Either way, it is all a part of His perfect plan, in His perfect love, in His perfect time for us.

It is never too late to get on track with God. Tapping into your ideal growth progression picks up where you are right now. No matter where you are in life or how old you are, God did not change His mind. There may have been a delay because of not following His path or hearing His voice. Don't let that stop you from starting now. Any experience you've gained along the way will be used to help someone in the time of your purpose.

Everything that we experience and learn is for a purpose. As we discover our gifts and learn to apply ourselves to developing and maturing in those gifts, we know these gifts will be used for a purpose. At some point in time, the season comes in our lives that causes us to be pushed into the right place, the place where all the experience, skills, knowledge, and more so, the gifting that you have are needed. And you will find at that time that you are perfectly equipped to do what God has created you to do.

There is a time for your purpose. Do not waste your effort trying to be noticed. If you rush to be noticed or if you are pushed into that place or position at the wrong time, outside of your season, God only knows what kind of results, delays, or damage it will cause. Be patient. Remember that song that says, "What God has for me, it is for me." I believe that if you are diligent and disciplined enough to follow the path that God has prepared for you, in the time for your purpose—no matter what that purpose is—it will be fulfilled in God.

Twelve

GET IN LINE FOR THE BLESSING

We often give people a parting salutation by telling someone to "be blessed." That doesn't mean to go get blessed; that means go *become a blessing* to someone else. Your purpose in God is directly tied to *you being* a blessing to someone else! When people ask how it's going, a lot of Christians say, "Oh, I'm blessed and highly favored." But what I say is, *"I'm blessed, and I can't help it."*

Believe it or not, there were times in my life that I really did try to "help it," so to speak. I lived a lifestyle that tried to derail God's plan for my life—it was a very destructive lifestyle. But thank God, He rescued me before it was too late. And it's not too late for you either.

Let me give you my logic or philosophies, or whatever you want to call it, behind the statement that says "I'm blessed and can't help it." I call it *"getting in line for the blessing."* Before I explain it, let me give you a couple of examples of real experiences I've had with getting in line for the blessing.

GEE GEE

Gee Gee is friend of mine who worked for the same company I worked for. She is ordained as a prophetess. She is someone that has been mightily used by God. She has frequently traveled internationally with some pretty well-known ministries. She is known to have a very different anointing when she travels abroad than she does stateside. In her travels, God has performed many signs and wonders through her. Let me tell you how God arranged for her to accept her calling and transformation. When God wants to reach someone, He'll do it by whatever method he chooses. Ask Jonah, who had a fish submarine for three days! But remember, these incidents are only a small piece of God's divine will in our lives.

Word got around the company where we worked that we had started a prayer group and a Bible class during lunchtime. Gee Gee heard about it and decided to come see what it was all about. This was kind of a stretch for her because, although she was a lifelong church member, she ran the lunchtime casino in the break room at work, where they would have many card games going on every day. She was a member of what I would call a different kind of church.

Gee Gee began to visit the Bible class periodically, and one day she told me that one of the church groups that she was involved in was having a program, and she wanted me to be the guest speaker. Mind you, at the time I had never spoken in a service outside of my own church. Plus I had heard about the reputation of this type of church, so I politely declined the offer. She boldly told me, "I figured you would say that." She began to tell me, "When I told the other people in my group, they said you would not be speaking for us. Plus, they said no one comes in there unless our pastor, Pastor Blue, brings them in. And if he doesn't know them, he never lets anybody in." Then Gee Gee kind of defiantly told me, "Well, I don't care what anyone says—God told me you would be the speaker, and that's all I know." I told her, "Well, if that's the case, He'd surely have to tell me and find a way to make that happen."

Well, here's the short version of what happened. About a week later, my pastor asked me to go to a pastors' luncheon with him on Saturday. It was being hosted by a well-known pastor in the area who was a friend of my pastor. We got to the luncheon, and we found that Richard Roberts, president of Oral Roberts University (ORU), was the guest speaker for the day. He told an interesting story about some kids who wanted to attend his school and that he was out raising money for their education.

See, these kids were poor but were saved in a revival. I believe it was somewhere in Texas. God told them to go to ORU to get their education. So they hitchhiked to Tulsa, Oklahoma, and began having prayer and worship on the street corners around the school. They made such an uproar that people began to notice and talk about it. When it was brought to Roberts's attention, he called them in, and they told him their story. He told them he couldn't help them. The school was in much debt, and they would have to leave and figure out a way to get money if they were to attend his school. Of course, they went back to having prayer and worship around the school.

As Richard Roberts was trying to figure out what to do about these kids, he told us that at some point in his prayer time, God told him to help those kids. He asked God, "How?" God told him to go to the major cities and ask the pastors to help and donate to their cause. Guess which city he came to first: Chicago!

So I attended this luncheon with my pastor, and before Roberts started telling us this story, an older gentleman walked up to our table saying he noticed an empty chair and asked if we minded if he joined us. We all exchanged pleasantries. He extended his hand to me and said, "Hello, my name is Pastor Blue." I nearly fell out of my chair!

Once the luncheon ended, Pastor Blue proceeded to tell us how much he enjoyed the company and conversations with some younger pastors like us. Before he left, I asked him if he knew Gee Gee and knew that I worked with her. He said yes and proceeded to tell me about how he'd known her and her family for many years. He seemed excited about it. So I reluctantly proceeded to mentioned that she had invited me to his church...as a guest...to speak!

He was one of these guys that always made emphasis with a long drawl. Boy, was I shocked at his response. He said, "Why suuure, any of you guys would be welcome at aaany time. I'd love to have you over to speak, by all means."

So the night came when I spoke at their church. Needless to say, it wasn't my great preaching nor my wonderful charisma that had an affect that night, considering only one person responded to the altar call, even though we really were glad and rejoiced in the one. But something else happened that we didn't expect. Within the following week, Gee Gee went through a complete transformation, left that church, and went on to become a real crusader for Christ.

There's a lot more to this story, but the point here is that God used some kids in Texas to get to Richard Roberts in Tulsa Oklahoma, which led a gathering of some pastors in Chicago, which led to my pastor inviting me to the lunch, which led to getting Pastor Blue and me seated at the same table, which led to me getting permission to speak at his church, which finally led to getting Gee Gee her transformation to pursue God's purpose.

Again, this is just my perspective, and I don't know what God's plan is for everyone in that line or what role this had in their destinies, but I do know of two people who were really blessed by it. Praise God!

GREGORY GREG

Greg, as we called him, was a man that touched the lives of our whole church. He was not a Christian. As a matter of fact, he was agnostic and grumpy! He brought his wife to the women's meeting that we have on Wednesday nights. As he was hanging around to wait for her, women that were there told him, "The men are meeting upstairs; you can't hang around here with the women." He came upstairs where the men were going over the lesson for the night. When we broke off into small groups, he was in my group. He sat observing the conversation, and then I asked him what he thought. After engaging him and getting him to open up, I found that we had similar backgrounds and careers. After I reminded the men to register for the men's retreat, which was starting that Friday, he asked if he could come to the men's retreat.

To make a long story short, he came to the retreat and gave his life to the Lord. The next day at the retreat, he was baptized in a spontaneous baptism in the lake where we were. That same afternoon, he received the full baptism of the Holy Spirit. He became a really solid member of our church, working with the security team, assisting in services, helping every way he could. He even did some of the cooking for our men's breakfast a few months later. We have small groups in our church, and Greg was trained as a group leader so he could start a group training young men in auto mechanic skills. Eleven months later, we were preparing for our next men's retreat, and Greg had a heart attack and died. This shook the whole church. He wife, Phyllis, was so appreciative of his assurance to make it into heaven. She said before he came to that retreat, their marriage was really struggling, but after his salvation, they had a better marriage than she could have ever imagined. She thanked the men and said, "If it had not been for the men in the church, he may not have made it in heaven."

GET IN LINE FOR THE BLESSING!
What am I saying here? In both of these stories, there were people involved that were totally unrelated to the resulting blessings that ensued. Nor were any of them aware of the outcome of their actions. As a matter of fact, they had no idea that they were in line for delivering a blessing or lined up for a blessing. As a result, my estimate is that thousands of people were actually blessed. Notice that all of the people in these

two stories heard God and followed His lead, and He orchestrated the rest. But He had to have people that were obedient to His voice.

When God gets ready to bless someone or perform a miracle, He uses people to deliver that blessing or miracle. He lines things up where the delivery is right on time. He uses one person to get it started, He may use another person to provide one thing and another person or persons to provide something else, and just in the nick of time, *bam*—a miracle happens for someone. I look at it like this: when God aims His blessing or miracle at someone, He has to have all the people who will deliver the blessings in mind also. That means He is mindful that persons A, B, C, and D will hear His voice, obey Him, and follow His direction, sometimes not even knowing that they are "in line." If you are one of those persons, just think—He is thinking about you! I believe that once that blessing is delivered, *every person in the line gets a blessing!*

This is where I say that math doesn't make sense—because when the blessing is delivered and the residual blessings to everyone in line are dispersed, the sum of all the parts is greater than the whole. God is a God of multiplication. The sum of the blessings of the people in line is probably greater than the blessing that was delivered. And in both cases, the blessings we received were exponentially higher than the effort put forth to deliver those blessings. The people in line are probably people that God knows are in the habit of blessing others. Better yet, how I say it is, *"I am in the blessing business."*

We, just like Jesus, are in the blessing business. When

my wife and I bless people, they say, "You guys really are a blessing." Or they may say, "You guys are really blessed." And what do we do after that? We just say "Amen, give God all the glory," or "Thank you, in Jesus's name!" Not just because it sounds good, but because they just added a blessing to our lives, and *we agreed*. Since I believe we have what we say and believe so much in the power of agreement, we just agreed that we are blessed. And since we're in the blessing business and many call us blessed, we are *blessed!*

"Again I say unto you, that if two of you shall agree on earth as touching any thing that they shall ask, it shall be done for them of my Father which is in heaven. For where two or three are gathered together in my name, there am I in the midst of them" (Mt 18:19–20).

When my siblings and I were growing up, because of our parents, we had many connections and relationships with a lot people. As we've gotten older, we realize how important those relationships are, the many lessons we've learned from them, and how important it is to be a blessing to everyone we meet. It is those relationships and blessings that are a reflection of who God created us all to be...which is a reflection of Him!

So when we make new acquaintances or reconnect with old ones, what face are we reflecting? Instead of reflecting a false image of a person who has an identity crisis and has no idea of who he or she is, let's allow our faces to stand behind the person we really are and not be judged by the look or image we're trying to portray. But let the true man that God created in His own image be the reflection that we give.

If we want people to know who we really are, then let's let our faces reflect our hearts.

So I say to you, *be blessed,* because you are a blessing!

We thank you, Lord Jesus, for what You have done,
For the battles that have been fought and already won.
We thank You for what you are going to do,
For all of these things You already foreknew.
We thank You, Lord Jesus, again and again.
Let everyone say, "Amen, amen."

Author: Holy Spirit
To Ellis McCarthy

ACKNOWLEDGEMENT

I thank my God and Savior Jesus Christ for wisdom, insight and experiences. Thank you for allowing me to recognize and articulate the things you have shown me; for developing me as a man.

Thank you to each person who's had an impact in my life and ministry. Thank you for your special relationships, encouragement, prayers and support. These were the necessary components that contributed to me successfully completing this book; I could not have done it without you.

Special thanks goes to:
Heavenly Enterprise for your coaching, editing and publishing expertise.

David Ellison and Peter Payne, men I look up to for perspective, which makes me look forward to tomorrow. The late Apostle Theodore Wilkinson for the years of friendship, and for leading me to lead men. In the early days, you saw more in me than I could see in myself. You didn't know the fire you ignited or the distance it would go.

Men of Christian Life Center, for pushing me to push you.

Andre Coker for sticking in there when others doubted Alex Zak, my Jewish brother from another mother, for the long talks and sharing our heritage and hearts.

To my siblings with whom I've lived, loved, fought, handheld and walked shoulder to shoulder through this life, sharing our love and our legacy.

Samula McCarthy, sister, student, co-laborer and inspiration.

Leonard McCarthy, brother, my biggest early life influence.

Dr. Dion McCarthy, brother, COGIC pastor, the carrier of the great mantle.

Joreece Mackie and Lorna Townes, sisters (deceased), whom I will forever love and look forward to seeing again.

WHY THIS BOOK? WHY NOW?

A successful man is one who lives in the center of God's will. This book will tell you where you are right now and, no less important, how to get to that exact spot where God wants you to be at this stage of your life.

William Arévalo, Campus Pastor
Christian Life Center, Blue Island

•

The blueprint for manhood is a must read. Ellis's lessons on the stages of life are powerful revelations on how to find your purpose and make a difference in a world that is in desperate need of male heroes. If you are lost and in need of a compass to guide you, this book is for you.

Pastor Tony Gilmore
St. Louis Dream Center

Ellis McCarthy has been instructing men of all ages, including myself, for years upon years. I am so excited that he has gathered all his thoughts, revelations, and life lessons and compiled them into a revolutionary read to help men navigate the different seasons of life. Blueprint of a God Man is sure to help many become the men God has designed them to be.

Sam Hamstra, Campus Pastor
Christian Life Center, Northwest Indiana

•

We are reminded through the passage of Ecclesiastes three, that timing is of utmost importance. To this I add, the timing of the Lord is e-v-e-r-y-t-h-i-n-g! As we live in a nation whose senior leadership and government supports men not just loving men, but men marrying men ... this writing is of utmost relevance to this moment in time. For this cause, I highly recommend Ellis McCarthy's newest book, "Blueprint of a God Man: Men Navigating the Seasons of Life."

Who better to create and then articulate the Heart of Father God, in relation to the awesome creation of His sons! The "Blueprint of a God Man" would most adroitly come from a man who is living his own life, according to the blueprint God has given unto him. In this premiere writing, Ellis challenges men to arise to a "them" that is greater than anything "they" have ever been. He presents thoughtful, provocative, life-changing principles that will work, if applied in truth. As he shares his heart, as he tells his story ... every man reading is ensconced to arise from wherever he is to live better, do better and be better to fulfill his destiny.

Ellis has always been a man of specificity, even when he did not realize it. Having known him since the mid-70's, I have had ample joy and opportunity to watch his life both up close, then later, from a distance. Despite the varied views afforded to me, I yet arrive at the very same point of vision ... this man is sent by God to the world in which we live! His candor mixed with the agape love of God, affords him the ability to confront, clarify, address and then bless the very lives he comes to strengthen.

As at no other time in history, men need to receive complete biblical blueprints that reflect the total truth of who they were created to be. Ellis possesses the innate ability to speak life, even to things that appear to be dead. This life-speaking wisdom arises not just from his brilliance and human intellect. His hearts' cry stems from his passion to see men be made whole, ergo his purpose is to communicate the God-created meaning of a man ... to a man. Spiritual, intuitive and holistic, this book will produce strength, healing and maturity in the lives of men, who hunger for more in their lives.

Every vehicle now sold, includes navigation. If a car possesses the ability to assess direction, how much more the lives of men? As Magellan launched out, knowing there was more than what his eyes could see, so must our world know that men can be changed to better navigate their personal seasons of life. Follow this purveyor who provides wisdom, insight and new blueprints to further aid men to be ALL they can be.

Apostle Nina-Marie
Founder and Senior Visionary
Speaking The Word Only Ministries, Inc.

I have the privilege of watching Ellis McCarthy lead men every week to a better relationship with God. It's a front row seat to the live version of the book that you are about to read. Without exception, I believe the experiences and truths you read will not only inspire and challenge you, but will set many free. I pray that you take the time to allow the inspired words of God spoken through the heart and hand of Ellis to encourage you to be a better husband, a better father, and a better son.

Ben Stewart
Christian Life Center, Tinley Park